ELIZABETH I

❀ the People's Queen ❀

ELIZABETH I

❀ the People's Queen ❀

Her Life and Times

21 Activities

KERRIE LOGAN HOLLIHAN

CHICAGO
REVIEW
PRESS

LIBRARY OF CONGRESS CATALOGING-IN-PUBLICATION DATA

Hollihan, Kerrie Logan.

  Elizabeth I—the people's queen : her life and times : 21 activities / Kerrie Logan Hollihan. — 1st ed.

    p. cm.

  Includes bibliographical references and index.

  ISBN 978-1-56976-349-0 (pbk.)

  1. Elizabeth I, Queen of England, 1533–1603—Juvenile literature. 2. Great Britain—History—Elizabeth, 1558–1603—Juvenile literature. 3. Queens—Great Britain—Biography—Juvenile literature. 4. Great Britain—Social life and customs—16th century—Study and teaching—Activity programs. 5. Great Britain—History—16th century—Study and teaching—Activity programs. 6. Creative activities and seat work—Juvenile literature. I. Title.

    DA355.H58 2011

    942.05′5092—dc22

    [B]

                                                                            2010047647

Cover and interior design: Monica Baziuk

Interior illustrations: Mark Baziuk

Cover images: (front cover, clockwise from upper left) Traitors' Gate and William Shakespeare © iStockphoto; Elizabeth on horseback from *Book of Faulconrie* by George Turbevile; *Elizabeth I, the Armada Portrait* attributed to George Gower, © The Gallery Collection/Corbis; sixpence and the ship *Henry Grace of God* © iStockphoto § (back cover, clockwise from upper right) *A Marriage Feast at Bermondsey* by Joris Hoefnagel; Court of King Henry VIII © iStockphoto/wynnter; embroidery by Martha Dillow, The Embroiders' Guild of America; Queen's champion courtesy Royal College of Arms

Tudor royal dynasty commemorative stamp designs on page 8 © Royal Mail Group Ltd. Reproduced by kind permission of Royal Mail Group Ltd. All rights reserved.

First edition

Published by Chicago Review Press, Incorporated

814 North Franklin Street

Chicago, Illinois 60610

ISBN 978-1-56976-349-0

Printed in the United States of America

5 4 3 2 1

To Bill, who helps make my writing life possible.

You may have many a wiser
prince sitting in this seat,
but you never have had,
or shall have,
any who loves you better.

—Queen Elizabeth I of England

CONTENTS

TIME LINE

1533 ◆ On September 7, Princess Elizabeth Tudor is born
to King Henry VIII and Queen Anne Boleyn

1536 ◆ Anne Boleyn is executed for treason
King Henry marries Jane Seymour two weeks later

1537 ◆ Princess Elizabeth is declared a bastard and removed from the royal line of succession

1547 ◆ Henry VIII dies and Elizabeth's half brother becomes King Edward VI
Elizabeth is sent to live with her stepmother, Katherine Parr

1551 ◆ Elizabeth returns as a member of Edward's court

1553 ◆ Edward dies and is succeeded by Lady Jane Grey until deposed by Elizabeth's sister Mary Tudor
Mary Tudor becomes queen of England

Elizabeth is imprisoned in the Tower of London for suspected plotting against Mary ◆ **1554**

Queen Mary dies after a bloody reign of persecution ◆ **1558**

Elizabeth is crowned England's Queen Elizabeth I ◆ **1559**

Elizabeth's cousin Mary Stuart returns from France to rule the Kingdom of Scotland ◆ **1561**

Elizabeth cancels a royal meeting with Mary, Queen of Scots, and they never meet ◆ **1562**

Elizabeth's soldiers defeat Catholic nobles during the Rising of the North ◆ **1569**

Elizabeth's spies uncover the Ridolfi plot to murder Elizabeth and replace her with Mary, Queen of Scots ◆ **1571**

Elizabeth sends Sir Francis Drake on his voyage around the world ◆ **1577**

Sir Walter Raleigh names a New World colony Virginia in honor of Elizabeth, the Virgin Queen ◆ **1584**

After being found guilty of conspiracy to kill Elizabeth, Mary, Queen of Scots, is executed on Elizabeth's order ◆ **1587**

The English navy defeats the Spanish Armada ◆ **1588**
Robert Dudley, Elizabeth's close friend and probable love of her life, dies

Elizabeth orders the execution of her young admirer, Robert Devereux, for treason ◆ **1601**

Elizabeth dies, leaving no successor ◆ **1603**
King James VI of Scotland becomes King James I of England

PREFACE

The World's a Stage

IN DECEMBER 1599, all was aflutter at the court of Elizabeth I, the queen of England. Her Majesty was looking forward to a quiet Christmas Day, followed by a dozen days of merrymaking with the lords and ladies who spent winter with her at Whitehall Palace on the Thames River. In these dark days of December and January, when there were only eight hours of daylight, everyone liked to party.

Elizabeth's Lord Chamberlain, who oversaw the queen's giant household of 300 courtiers (political friends and allies and assorted hangers-on who attended the queen) and 1,200 servants, had orders to hire musicians and entertainers for the court's revels. There were 12 nights to think of, and he needed to plan for music and dancing and plays. He met with an actors' group, the Lord Chamberlain's Men, to talk about an assignment. They were to write and perform a play to entertain Elizabeth and her guest, an Italian duke.

The performance would take place on January 6, the Feast of the Epiphany, when Christians honored the visit of the Wise Men to the baby Jesus. Elizabeth and her court also celebrated this date as Twelfth Night, the final night of fun that capped the Twelve Days of Christmas.

The actors got together, making haste as they set their plans. Dame Fortune—good luck—smiled on them. One of the actors was a gifted playwright, a man from Stratford named William Shakespeare.

With just a few days to go before Christmas, Shakespeare sat down at a wooden table with his quill pen, ink, and a sheaf of papers in front of him. There he wrote *Twelfth Night*, a comedy about mixed-up people living in a fantasy world. One of the characters took his name from the queen's Italian visitor.

William Shakespeare went on to become the English language's best-known playwright.

Queen Elizabeth I and her court enjoyed Shakespeare's plays in the Globe Theatre.

Shakespeare understood how people think and act as they live their lives, and he wrote about human nature in his plays and poems. As he said in his play *As You Like It*:

All the world's a stage,
And all the men and women merely players;
They have their exits and their entrances.

Shakespeare and the rest of the Lord Chamberlain's Men went on stage before Queen Elizabeth on January 6, 1600. He may well have wondered about the queen. Elizabeth, though dressed in a gown heavy with jewels and embroidery, was showing her years. The queen was heavily painted with white makeup, but Shakespeare could see the lines etched on her face. They marked a long and complex life.

Queen Elizabeth's very life was high drama. Surrounding her was a cast of characters—kings, queens, lords, ladies, heroes, villains, gentlemen, gentlewomen, soldiers, sailors, and ordinary English folk. Like Shakespeare's actors, they made their entrances and exits as Elizabeth's drama unfolded.

Each man and woman, together with the queen, played against a bold, brutal backdrop.

William Shakespeare's characters have stayed famous for more than 400 years. These trading cards came in packages of tea sold in the early 1900s.

Queen Elizabeth I of England.
Library of Congress LC-USZ62-47605

In the 1500s, there were wars among Europe's feuding nations about how to worship God. But amid this setting of strife and blood, there was good news: the rise of a tiny island nation called England during the Age of Elizabeth.

A Princess Unwanted

THE MIDWIFE must have groaned. Praise God for Queen Anne's safe delivery in childbed, but this new baby was a maid, not the lusty boy King Henry had been promised. As the midwife displayed the baby girl to the crowd of people in the queen's chamber, they knew the queen had failed. She had not borne the heir to England's throne, the son her husband longed for.

Still, the baby girl's arrival signaled the start of a celebration. It was September 7, 1533. England had a new princess, first in line to the throne. As the news flowed out of Greenwich Palace and up the Thames River to London, people poured out of their houses to make merry. King Henry VIII and his new queen, Anne Boleyn (boe-LIN), had a healthy child. Surely a son would follow in God's—and King Henry's—good time.

With her mother still in bed, where she would stay for a month to recover from the birth, the baby girl was taken to a church in Greenwich. There she was christened with great pomp and style. One of the king's men shouted her name: "God of his infinite goodness, send prosperous life and long to the high and mighty princess of England, Elizabeth!"

But in a different household, another English princess refused to celebrate. She was Mary Tudor, 17 years old and daughter of Henry VIII with his first wife, Queen Catherine of Aragon. The new baby meant only bitterness to Mary. When her mother could not give Henry a son, he dropped her for the pretty, dark-haired Anne Boleyn. Henry's wandering eye had spotted Anne, one of Queen Catherine's ladies at court.

Under the rules of the Roman Catholic Church, Henry could not divorce his wife. So Henry split from the Catholic Church. The king created a new Protestant religion, the Church of England, and he made himself its supreme head. Now Henry made the laws. He divorced Queen Catherine and packed her off to a home in the country, where she and her servants lived in disgrace.

Under the king's new rules, Mary became Henry's illegitimate daughter, a bastard child not born in a legal marriage. Henry stripped away Mary's title of princess. The king's older daughter became simply Lady Mary. Her claim to England's throne came second to baby Elizabeth's.

ABOVE: Queen Anne Boleyn, Princess Elizabeth's mother, was executed when Elizabeth was two.
LEFT: King Henry VIII of England, Princess Elizabeth's father, married six wives. Two he divorced, two he executed, one died, and the last outlived him. © iStockphoto/wynnter

A Home at Hatfield

WHEN ELIZABETH was just three months old, King Henry gave her an estate of her own with caregivers and servants. Elizabeth was taken

✤ Create Your Family's Coat of Arms

QUEEN ELIZABETH'S coat of arms, as well as those of noble families in her court, had their roots in the Middle Ages. Knights in combat wore head-to-toe armor and needed a symbol so that other soldiers could identify them. These symbols appeared on the armor and also on a simple shirt that covered the armor to protect it from rust. These became known as coats of arms.

Through the years, these symbols evolved into intricate designs showing a shield and helmet topped by a crest in the family colors. Often they appear with a family motto written on a scroll. You can design a coat of arms for your family and write your own family motto as well.

You'll Need
- ✤ Paper
- ✤ Pencil
- ✤ Markers
- ✤ Scissors

Photocopy the pattern on this page to create a full-sized pattern of the shield, helmet, and motto.

Think about what makes you proud of your family. What

do you want the world to see on your coat of arms? Coats of arms show all kinds of things: castles, dragons, stars, seashells, arrows, hearts, lions, griffins, crowns, bees, and ships. Depending on what you wish to include, divide your shield in half or in quarters and draw pictures in each space. Then, brainstorm your family motto.

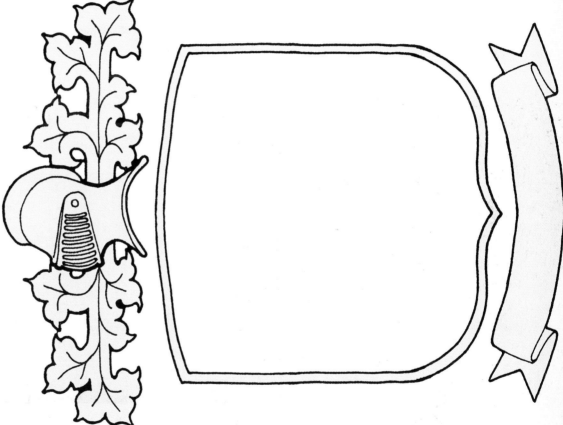

As a queen and head of state, Elizabeth had a complex coat of arms. The three lions shown on two quarters of the shield came from King Richard I, known as Richard the Lionhearted. The other two quarters bear the *fleur de lis*, the lily of France, reflecting King Edward III's claim on the French throne.

to Hatfield, a royal manor home west of London. There, following the customs of the day, the little girl was raised in the manner befitting a princess. Her mother Queen Anne stayed at court, no doubt in the hope that she would quickly become pregnant with a son for King Henry.

Surrounded by noble ladies of high birth, common servants, and wet nurses who breast-fed the little princess, baby Elizabeth thrived at Hatfield. Her sister Mary lived at Hatfield as well; the king had ordered her to serve as one of Elizabeth's ladies.

But Mary refused to acknowledge Elizabeth's royal birth. By insisting that she alone was England's princess, Mary outraged her father. Over the years, the distance between King Henry and his eldest daughter grew, as did Mary's dislike of her small sister.

Queen Anne did her best to produce an heir for King Henry. She miscarried one baby and then, in the winter of 1535, she gave birth to a stillborn son. By then, Henry's eyes had landed

LEFT: This fashion illustration shows King Henry VIII standing with key players in his family. From left to right are Queen Anne Boleyn, Henry VIII, Queen Jane Seymour, Queen Katherine Parr (seated), Princess Elizabeth Tudor, Prince Edward Tudor, and Princess Mary Tudor. This scene existed only in the artist's imagination. © iStockphoto/wynntera RIGHT: Hatfield House, where Princess Elizabeth grew up.

✿ Write Your Name in Your Own Typeface

THE PRINTED word can appear in many forms, called typefaces or fonts. When graphic designers plan the layout of a book, they choose typefaces that fit the book's subject. The typeface you are reading is named Nexus Sans. Now look at the printing on page 4. It has a different look. Its name is Requiem.

When early printing presses came about in the mid-1400s, typesetters placed each letter of type by hand. At first, typefaces mimicked the hand-printed calligraphy of medieval monks. When Johannes Gutenberg printed his first Bible in 1455, it appeared in a heavy typeface that looked like manuscript writing.

As designers put their own ideas to work creating typefaces, the art of typography was born. Often these designs echo the time in history when their designers were working.

The Declaration typeface brings the Declaration of Independence to mind.

`Courier was used on typewriter keys.`

Now it's your turn to become a graphic designer.

You'll Need
✿ Writing paper
✿ Pencil or pen
✿ Ruler

Start by studying some of the typefaces printed below.

Think: which typeface looks older to you? Study the letters in the examples on this page. See how the uppercase letters and lowercase letters resemble each other. Note how parts of each letter are long or short, thick or thin. Do you like serifs? How should your typeface look?

Now print your full name in big plain letters on the paper. Start to play around with the letters. It might be easier to start with the capitals first. Or start with all capitals—some fonts are designed that way.

Take your time. Every so often, sit back and look at your work. Do the letters work together in an artistic way?

Keep practicing until your name looks just right in your new typeface.

The Mayflower typeface recalls Elizabethan England.

Century Schoolbook type appeared in children's literature.

The Franklin Caslon typeface brings Benjamin Franklin and colonial America to mind.

This typeface is Baskerville. Baskerville is a "serif" typeface. Serifs are small curlicues on the tips of letters.

ABCDEFGHIJKLM
NOPQRSTUVWXYZ
abcdefghijklmn
opqrstuvwxyz

This typeface is Kievit. Kievit is a "sans-serif" typeface. The serifs have disappeared.

ABCDEFSGHIJKLM
NOPQRSTUVWXYZ
abcdefghijklmn
opqrstuvwxyz

on several choices for a new queen. He plotted ways to rid himself of Queen Anne and replace her with his new favorite, one of Anne's ladies named Jane Seymour.

Henry's courtiers accused Anne of betraying the king with other men. Anne was removed from the royal household, placed on a boat, and rowed along the Thames River to the forbidding Tower of London, where she entered prison through Traitors' Gate.

Anne tried to defend herself against these false charges, but King Henry was determined.

Found guilty of treason—disloyalty to both her king and country—Anne was condemned to be beheaded. Anne was a member of the nobility, so her sentence was carried out in private on Tower Green, a grassy patch inside the walls of the Tower of London. Henry brought in a French executioner, the most skilled swordsman he could find. As a woman, Anne was entitled to die by the sword instead of an ax.

The executioner did his work perfectly. At eight o' clock in the morning on May 19, 1536, he beheaded Anne with one swift stroke.

LEFT: **Highborn prisoners were jailed in the Tower of London, already 500 years old when Elizabeth was a girl.** Library of Congress LC-DIG-ppmsc-08566
RIGHT: **A headman's ax and execution block stand on display in the Tower of London.**
Library of Congress LC-USZ61-922

Nobody had thought about a coffin, so her ladies took her head and body and placed them together in an old arrow box. By noon, the box had been buried under the floor of the chapel just steps away.

Now, two-year-old Elizabeth became both motherless and a bastard. As with her sister Mary, Elizabeth was stripped of her title by King Henry. Before Anne Boleyn's body was barely cold, Henry became betrothed to Lady Jane Seymour. Queen Jane became Henry's third wife and little Elizabeth's stepmother. The new queen gave King Henry his longed-for male heir. On October 12, 1537, Prince Edward Tudor was born.

The king ordered Elizabeth and Mary to Hampton Court Palace so they could take part in the christening ceremony. Only four, Elizabeth was too small to carry a fancy cloth for the ceremony. A nobleman scooped her up and held Elizabeth as she grasped the jeweled fabric in her small hands. Elizabeth looked on as prayers were offered for the health and long life of her baby half brother.

Queen Jane was not blessed with a long life. Like so many women in her day, she developed a massive infection after giving birth to Edward and died 12 days later.

Henry VIII went on to marry three more wives by the time Elizabeth turned 10. A princess from the Netherlands, Anne of Cleves,

arrived to marry the king in 1539, but Henry found her so plain he divorced her and sent her to the countryside.

Henry's next wife, yet another pretty girl from court named Catherine Howard, liked Elizabeth and sent her small trinkets. But the hapless Catherine truly did cheat on the king and was beheaded on Tower Green in 1542 when Elizabeth was nine. At long last, King Henry, now old and sick, settled on an older woman named Katherine Parr and married her in the summer of 1543.

Elizabeth tried to please her father and his new wife. Following the Tudor custom of exchanging gifts at New Year, she made her stepmother a handmade book. In it, Elizabeth labored with pen and ink to translate a French poem into English. Instead of using the Old English style of writing, Elizabeth wrote with a new kind of penmanship, the Italic style so fashionable in Italy. Then she took up needle and thread to embroider a cover for the little book.

Princess Elizabeth handwrote a prayer book for her stepmother, Katherine Parr, and embroidered the cover in silk thread with the queen's initials. Elizabeth made the book as a New Year's gift. People did not exchange gifts at Christmas as they do now.

A Princess Once More

IN 1543, Elizabeth's future brightened. Henry VIII, a whimsical man, changed his mind about his daughters' low position. Henry rewrote his will and reversed his shocking decision to remove his daughters' royal titles. Mary, now 28, and Elizabeth, 10, again became Tudor princesses.

King Henry was trying to plan for the future. If his son Edward died without fathering children, first Mary and then Elizabeth would follow their brother on England's throne.

Under English law, sons always came first. Among England's noble families, the oldest son inherited his father's title and practically all of his land and buildings. Other sons and daughters could only hope that their father would leave them some land or cash to give them an income.

The same tradition held in England's royal family. The oldest son—and then his children—inherited the crown. If the oldest son died childless, the crown went to the next son—or daughter, if no sons were left. Even if a princess was older than her brother, she could not wear the crown before he did.

Elizabeth's family tree was an example of the royal succession. Her father Henry had an older brother, Arthur, who died in his teens. Henry then became first in line to the throne, though his sister Margaret was two years older.

The Reformation and a Europe Split in Two

QUEEN ELIZABETH's life played out against a bloody backdrop. The 1500s, a century of religious uproar, saw the Christian church splinter into groups that hated each other and went to war. They fought over land, power, and money.

As the 1500s opened, the Roman Catholic Church oversaw a religious empire across

A series of stamps shows the Tudor royal dynasty, which ruled England from 1485 to 1603. Royal Mail

HENRY VII 1485-1509   HENRY VIII 1509-1547   EDWARD VI 1547-1553   LADY JANE GREY 1553   MARY I 1553-1558   ELIZABETH I 1558-1603

Tudor Family Tree

Names printed in bold show the Tudors who
ruled England as kings and queens.

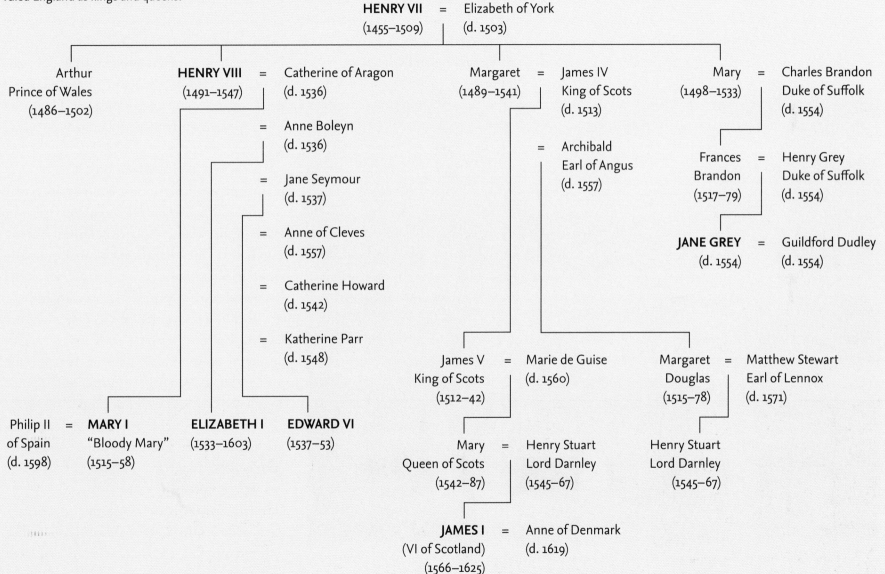

HENRY VII = Elizabeth of York
(1455–1509)   (d. 1503)

Arthur
Prince of Wales
(1486–1502)

HENRY VIII = Catherine of Aragon
(1491–1547)   (d. 1536)

= Anne Boleyn
(d. 1536)

= Jane Seymour
(d. 1537)

= Anne of Cleves
(d. 1557)

= Catherine Howard
(d. 1542)

= Katherine Parr
(d. 1548)

Margaret = James IV
(1489–1541)   King of Scots
(d. 1513)

= Archibald
Earl of Angus
(d. 1557)

Mary = Charles Brandon
(1498–1533)   Duke of Suffolk
(d. 1554)

Frances = Henry Grey
Brandon   Duke of Suffolk
(1517–79)   (d. 1554)

JANE GREY = Guildford Dudley
(d. 1554)   (d. 1554)

James V = Marie de Guise
King of Scots   (d. 1560)
(1512–42)

Margaret = Matthew Stewart
Douglas   Earl of Lennox
(1515–78)   (d. 1571)

Philip II = MARY I   ELIZABETH I   EDWARD VI
of Spain   "Bloody Mary"   (1533–1603)   (1537–53)
(d. 1598)   (1515–58)

Mary = Henry Stuart
Queen of Scots   Lord Darnley
(1542–87)   (1545–67)

Henry Stuart
Lord Darnley
(1545–67)

JAMES I = Anne of Denmark
(VI of Scotland)   (d. 1619)
(1566–1625)

Europe. At its head was the pope, who traced his authority back to St. Peter, a disciple of Jesus. From its seat of power in Rome, the Catholic Church wielded its enormous influence for 1,500 years over everyone in Western Europe.

The Church taught that it held power over people's souls, from humble peasants to kings and queens. Everyone must obey Catholic teachings and do good works during life on earth. Otherwise, a person's soul would go to the fires of hell.

Even then, living a righteous life might not be enough. Catholics taught that after death, a dead person's soul enters purgatory. There, the soul repented for bad deeds before earning its way into heaven.

In the early 1500s, the popes were busy planning a magnificent new church of St. Peter in Rome. The cathedral promised to be an extraordinary but expensive building. As they watched the new creation rise in Rome, the Church leaders found a way to pay for it by selling indulgences—"time off" from purgatory.

Greed and corruption had seeped into every level of the Church, from parish priests to bishops to the pope himself. Then, in 1517, a young priest named Martin Luther nailed a list of complaints on a church door in Wittenberg, Germany. Luther charged that Church leaders had fallen into this sorry mess by selling indulgences.

Luther had other shocking ideas. He claimed that faith alone—not good works—earns one's soul a place in heaven. Luther pointed out that Christ's church is a body of believers—both ordinary people as well as

This old painting shows the heroes of the Reformation. Martin Luther stands in the center holding his writings. Queen Elizabeth, one of a few women the artist included, stands to the left. Library of Congress LC-USZ61-922

priests. He declared that Church leaders such as the pope, bishops, and priests had no special lifeline to God. Luther kept only two of the seven Catholic holy sacraments: baptism and the Lord's Supper—communion. His views also changed the meaning of taking bread and wine at communion.

Soon Luther's reforms snowballed into a movement called the Reformation. Throughout the 1500s, Protestant ("protest"-ant) churches surged across northern Europe in a wave of Lutheranism. Many people approved of Luther's reforms and became Protestants. For better or worse, the new church attracted about 300 princes in northern Germany alone. They wanted to help themselves to the riches and influence of the Roman Catholic Church. But in southern Germany, Catholics continued to hold power.

King Henry VIII of England left the Catholic Church in the 1530s in order to get a divorce that the pope would not approve. Henry established his own form of a Protestant religion: the Church of England, or Anglican Church. In Switzerland, yet another branch of Protestants united under their leader, John Calvin, who taught that only special people, "the elect," were "predestined" to enter heaven.

This map shows how Europe looked when Elizabeth became queen.

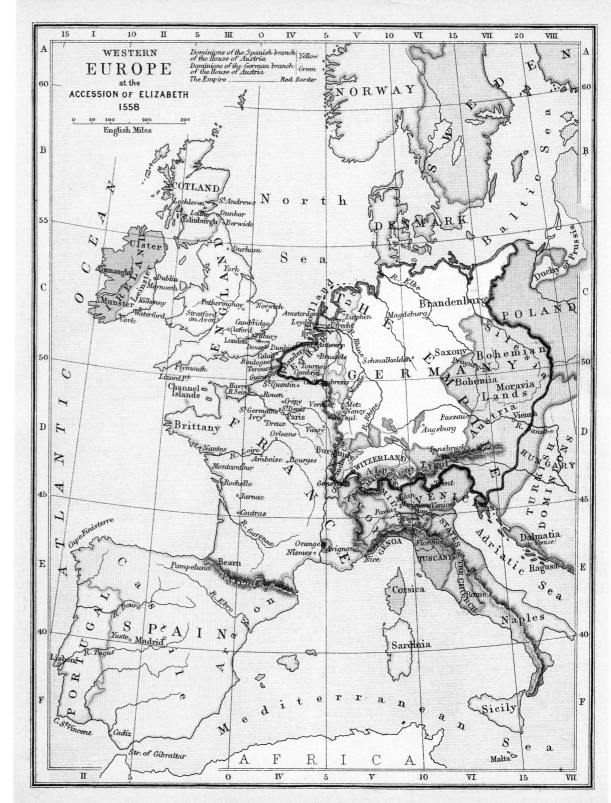

The Reformation laid the groundwork for bloody clashes in the 1500s. Nations took sides depending on which way their monarchs worshipped. Kings and queens signed treaties and married each other to cement the bonds of religion across national borders. When armies went to war, they took sides depending on whether they were Catholics or Protestants.

About the time Elizabeth became England's queen in 1558, Europe's map was divided in two. Under Elizabeth, England was Protestant. But much of the north of England was still friendly

Book burning has long been a way for people to try to destroy their opponents' ideas about God.

to Catholics, and farther north lay Catholic Scotland. To the west, Ireland was divided. English landowners in Ireland were Protestants, but their Irish enemies were Catholics.

In Northern Europe, including Scandinavia and Germany, kings and princes followed Protestant beliefs. In France, most kings and the occasional queen were Catholics, but French nobles also included Protestants, which led to infighting and murder. Germany remained a nation of princes divided between Protestants and Catholics. Members of Spain's royal family were strong Catholics, as were the monarchs of the Holy Roman Empire that spanned central Europe and parts of Holland, Belgium, and Italy. The princes of Italy kept their Catholic ways as well.

The lives of everyday people also played out against this backdrop. Protestants and Catholics feared each other. A small child's future depended on the family religion, and that family felt safer living near others with the same beliefs.

In cities and towns, a father's work and even the chance for his sons to go to school depended on how he worshipped as a Catholic or Protestant. In the countryside, families followed the religion practiced by the rich landowners who gave them work and shelter.

This split between religions set the stage for killing between Protestants and Catholics in Europe for more than a century. Elizabeth Tudor grew up during these days of war and revenge.

"No Womanly Weakness"

2

AS THE child of Henry VIII, Elizabeth had the best teachers in her father's kingdom. Even Elizabeth's governess, Mistress Katherine Ashley, was handpicked for her knowledge. Kat Ashley spent hours with the little princess each day and most likely taught Elizabeth how to read and write. Elizabeth began to learn Latin, the language of Europe's educated people.

For a time, Elizabeth and her brother Edward lived in the same home. Like some girls in rich families, Elizabeth was lucky to work with a tutor hired to teach her brother. Side by side, Edward and Elizabeth studied Latin and Greek, a newly popular subject for study and conversation. Elizabeth, however, did not study international politics and affairs of state as Edward did. No one dreamed that a young girl would need to understand these subjects.

The purest treasure mortal times afford
Is spotless reputation

—William Shakespeare, *Richard II*

Elizabeth loved learning. In a different place and time, she might well have become a scholar. By age 11 she was well into learning Greek, Latin, French, and Italian. Elizabeth took pride in her work, be it her penmanship, her stitchery, or her bookwork. As she neared her teens, she was growing into a smart and strong-willed young woman.

Elizabeth was delighted to get a tutor of her very own. But this teacher, a thoughtful man named William Grindal, soon died of the Black Death, a plague that attacked its victims with

ABOVE: Princess Elizabeth Tudor at age 14.

Library of Congress LC-USZ62-47605

RIGHT: This map of England, Scotland, and Ireland printed in 1570 looks sideways to modern eyes. The cartographer mapped it with "due West" on top and "due North" on the right side.

Library of Congress Maps Collection

✿ Cloak Yourself Like an Elizabethan

QUEEN ELIZABETH ordered men in her court to wear short cloaks. To the queen, this was a matter of safety. A long cloak would make an excellent hiding place for a pistol or knife. Ladies, however, kept their cloaks long.

You can make and wear a cloak like the well-dressed people of Elizabeth's court. Add a crisp white ruff (see page 47), and you will make a dandy Elizabethan!

Adult supervision required

You'll Need
✿ Partner
✿ Tape measure
✿ Soft fabric, such as fleece, knit, or felt, that will not unravel
✿ Sewing scissors or large, sharp craft scissors
✿ Chalk
✿ Brooch or pin from an old set of jewelry

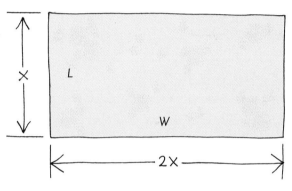

To begin, have your partner measure your cape length. This is the distance from the large bone in back of your neck to wherever you want the bottom of your cape to fall. Write down the measurement.

Cut a rectangular piece of fabric by following the diagram below. The width should be twice the cape length. For example, if your cape length is 40 inches, you must cut a piece of fabric that's 40 inches long and 80 inches wide.

Fold the fabric in half so that it makes a square. The fold of the fabric should run up the left side of the square.

Look at the diagram below. From the upper left-hand corner of the fabric, at the top of the fold, measure 4 inches in both directions and mark those spots with chalk. Then draw a gentle curve from one mark to the other, as shown.

Look at the lower right-hand corner of the fabric. Follow the example in the diagram and draw another curve.

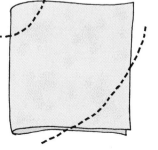

Now you are ready to cut out your cape. You will cut through both layers of fabric at once. See what happens when you unfold the fabric?

Place your cape around your neck. If you wish, fold over a bit of the cape to form a collar. Close it with the brooch or pin.

CAST OF CHARACTERS: *An English Schoolboy*

WILLIAM SHAKESPEARE looked back on childhood when he recalled

. . . the whining schoolboy, with his satchel
And shining morning face, creeping like snail
Unwillingly to school . . .

Shakespeare's broad knowledge of Latin and Greek showed he probably attended grammar school in Stratford. Boys like Will started at petty school, which blended religious education with language arts. Will studied the Book of Common Prayer to learn to read and write English.

At age six or seven, a boy started grammar school, where he spent long days—from 6:00 or 7:00 A.M. until 4:00 P.M. or even later. (Everyone took a dinner break and ate a big meal at midday.) There, he and his classmates learned to speak and write Latin. They read from the *King's Grammar*. This textbook presented problems because it gave the rules for writing Latin *in Latin*.

As a boy moved through lower and upper grammar school, he read the classic works of ancient Latin writers. By the time he was a teen, he learned some ancient Greek. Princess Elizabeth did her lessons by reading and trans- lating the same ancient texts as her brother did.

Like Elizabeth, English boys studied the art of rhetoric (REH-to-rik) to sharpen their skills at critical thinking. They learned to communicate ideas by writing clearly, as well as by making speeches that they wrote with care.

School bored most young pupils. For the most part, learning meant rote memorizing, saying the same things over and over until they burned into a boy's brain. Other times, school meant punishment. Arrive late for class, and a boy risked a beating from his schoolmaster, unless a kindly father sent along an invitation for the teacher to come to dinner.

On dark winter days, pupils grew stiff and cold sitting on benches with little to light their hornbooks, which were pieces of board mounted with printed texts and covered with thin slices of animal horn for protection. If a schoolboy spoke English instead of Latin, the master's stick on his back reminded him not to forget.

fever, vomiting, and black, blood-filled boils. A replacement was named, but he was not Elizabeth's first choice. Elizabeth, a hardheaded girl, had become a penpal—writing in Latin—with a teacher at Cambridge University named Roger Ascham (ASK-um). She would accept no one else, and when she was 16, Ascham joined her household for two years.

Elizabeth's intelligence astounded her new tutor. He eagerly wrote, "She has just passed her sixteenth birthday, and exhibits such seriousness and gentility as are unheard of in one of her age and rank."

Elizabeth's morning lessons began with readings from the Bible in its original Greek. Ascham then directed her to translate complex passages from Latin, Greek, and Italian into their original languages. Once she finished, Ascham asked her to translate them back into English—with no peeking until she was finished.

A well-taught pupil during the Renaissance studied other subjects as well. (Today,

Queen Elizabeth signed papers with an elaborate signature.

a Renaissance man or Renaissance woman means anyone with a wide range of interests and talent.) Ascham taught Elizabeth his own lovely penmanship in the Italian style, and Elizabeth learned to write in a fine hand that served her well through life.

Ascham also gave Elizabeth lessons in elocution. Public speaking was not the custom for girls. But Ascham saw brilliance in his star pupil; she was as strong a scholar as any prince.

Her study of true religion and learning is most energetic. . . . Her mind has no womanly weakness, her perseverance is equal to that of a man, and her memory long retains that which it readily grasps. . . . When she writes Greek and Latin, nothing is more beautiful than her handwriting. . . . She is as much delighted with music as she is skilful in that art. In adornment of person she aims at elegance rather than show . . . [with] contempt of gold and elaborate headdress.

Like her father, Elizabeth loved music. She was a skilled player of the lute, a long-necked instrument similar to a guitar, as well as the virginal, an early type of keyboard instrument.

Though a princess, Elizabeth did not dress elaborately. She took great care to choose simple, sober clothing, proper for a young Protestant woman. Catholic women might wear jewels and lace, but such finery did not befit a

In Tudor times, people "hawked" with falcons to catch other birds and animals.

Protestant. Elizabeth, of course, was a strong Protestant and member of the Church of England, the church which her father, the king, led.

Outdoors, Elizabeth built her skills in other Tudor pastimes. She learned to a ride a horse with ease and to join the hunt for deer and birds. She also enjoyed another royal hobby: hunting with falcons to catch small animals.

✿ Play and Sing a Madrigal

ELIZABETHANS OFTEN gathered to enjoy music, a popular way to spend time together. Some played the virginal, an early piano, and others strummed lutes, long-necked stringed instruments that looked a bit like guitars. Everyone joined in singing madrigals (MAD-ri-gals), the pop songs of their day. Sad songs were a huge hit among Elizabethans.

John Dowland, a gifted lutenist and songwriter, asked for a position at Queen Elizabeth's court but was refused because he was a Catholic. Dowland moved to Europe and worked for the king of Denmark. Catholics who plotted against Elizabeth tried to enlist Dowland to help them, but he refused.

Eventually Dowland won a position in the court of Elizabeth's successor, King James I, where people played and sang his mournful but very popular tunes. "Flow My Tears" is one. Will Shakespeare admired Dowland's music and referred to the song in his play *Twelfth Night*.

Try out Dowland's song for yourself. Practice playing it on the piano if you play, or else ask an accompanist to play, and then gather some friends to sing. You can find the piano music at www.kerrieloganhollihan.com.

BY THE 1530s, when Elizabeth was a child, England had entered the Renaissance. Scholars, mostly men but also a few women, dropped their medieval viewpoints and began to look at life in a modern way.

The Renaissance (REN-u-sans) came to northern Europe from Italy, where human society was experiencing a rebirth. Crusaders to the Holy Land in the 1200s and 1300s had brought back books and scrolls, parchment animal skins filled with the writing of Arab scholars who lived in the Middle East. Many of these documents held information more than 1,000 years old, writings from ancient Greece and Rome.

Much of this knowledge had been lost to Europe since the Roman Empire collapsed in 410 AD. Now there was much to discover. Greeks, Romans, and Arabs had written books on astronomy, mathematics, and medicine. There were ancient plays, myths, poems, and stories to unravel. Old texts told the history of Greece and Rome—even the history of Europe that the Romans themselves had written 1,400 years earlier.

In about 1437, Johannes Gutenberg invented the printing press, and knowledge took off like a rocket. The printing press meant one thing: information could be produced cheaply and distributed far and wide.

Once Europeans had books that linked them to ancient ideas, there was an explosion of things to study. Scholars scanned the sky with its wandering sun, moon, stars, and planets. They also took a deeper look into life on earth, its rocks, plants, animals, and birds. Above all, they began to focus on earth's most exalted creature, the human being.

To Renaissance people, God still ruled the universe, but here on earth, man (as people thought then) was in his glory. Nothing was more beautiful than the human form and the human mind, something for artists to paint and sculpt, for writers to explore, and for musicians to praise.

Elizabeth Tudor grew up immersed in the rich intellectual environment of the Renaissance. Thanks to her skills in literature, language, sport, dance, music, and handwriting, Elizabeth I became the world's best-known Renaissance woman.

The Renaissance painter Raphael captured the era's fascination with geometry in this painting of Greek mathematicians. © iStockphoto/estelle75

No One to Trust

IN 1546, Elizabeth and Mary were called to live with their father at court. One could wonder whether King Henry ever thought about Anne Boleyn when he gazed on his second daughter.

At 12, Elizabeth looked nothing like her dark-haired, dark-eyed mother. Elizabeth not only had her father's taste in music and gift for learning, she had inherited his strawberry red hair, as well. Average in height, slim, with pretty hands and long fingers, Elizabeth looked every inch a princess.

The following January, news rang out from Whitehall Palace: "The king is dead! Long live the king!" Henry VIII had breathed his last, and Edward, just a boy of nine, became King Edward VI. But Edward was too young for the job of ruling his country. Until he came of age at 21, England's government was in the hands of a lord protector, or temporary head of state. Eager for power, Edward's uncle Edward Seymour stepped into the position, surrounded by his circle of advisers, the Privy Council.

Henry VIII's widow, Katherine Parr, would not be a widow for long. Before she married Henry, Katherine had loved another nobleman, Thomas Seymour, a baron and the younger brother of the lord protector. Katherine married Seymour and invited Elizabeth to live with them at Katherine's home in Chelsea.

Katherine made a poor choice in marrying Seymour. Everyone knew that Seymour had hoped to marry Elizabeth but settled for Katherine Parr. Once Elizabeth moved to Chelsea, Seymour began to flirt with the young princess, who was at least 25 years younger than he. Seymour went so far as to enter Elizabeth's private chamber early in the mornings before she was up and dressed for the day. Katherine joined her husband on his visits and even joined him

Katherine Parr. © iStockphoto/Duncan Walker

✿ Stitch a Blackwork Flower

BLACKWORK WAS a favorite type of embroidery that Elizabethans used to decorate their clothes and household items. One by one, tiny black stitches grew into intricate designs. Portraits of Queen Elizabeth show examples of blackwork embroidery on her sleeves.

Blackwork is fun to do and easy to learn. All it takes is a needle and thread, an embroidery hoop, and one type of embroidery stitch called the backstitch. With

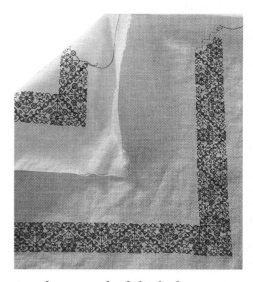

A modern example of Elizabethan blackwork. Martha Dillow, The Embroiderers' Guild of America

(continued on next page)

❀ Stitch a Blackwork Flower *(continued)*

some practice, you can stitch up flowers that Elizabethans grew.

You'll Need

- ❀ Black embroidery thread
- ❀ Embroidery needle
- ❀ Several 6-inch squares of 12-count Aida cross-stitch fabric
- ❀ 4-inch embroidery hoop
- ❀ Sewing pin
- ❀ Sewing pin
- ❀ Small, sharp scissors
- ❀ Ruler
- ❀ 1 piece cardstock
- ❀ Masking tape

First, learn the backstitch. Cut a piece of embroidery thread about 18 inches long. Thread the needle and tie a knot at one end. Leave a 3-inch tail hanging from the eye of needle. This will help you keep the thread from pulling out of the needle as you sew.

Practice the backstitch on scrap fabric by following the diagram below. Working from right to left:

Come up at hole 1. Take a stitch back to hole 2 and go in. Come back up at hole 3.

Hole 3 becomes your new hole 1, and the stitch repeats.

You can watch a lesson on backstitch at www.needlenthread.com/2006/10/embroidery-stitch-video-tutorial_24.html

Next, study your cross-stitch fabric. Do you see how the fabric has tiny holes? You will backstitch by

skipping your needle over two holes *under* the fabric but then stitch backward *over* one on top. That's why it's called backstitch!

When you start to run out of thread, turn the piece over and weave your needle through a few stitches. Cut off the remaining thread with small scissors, *but be careful not to cut the cloth.*

Now you are ready to stitch. Try the gillyflower first.

Before you start, look at the pattern and find the center. Now find the center of your fabric. Stitch the pattern so that it's centered on the fabric. Think: where will you start your stitching? Mark that spot with the pin.

Cut a piece of embroidery thread 18 inches long. Split the thread into six strands. You will use two strands at a time, so set the others aside for now. Thread both strands through the needle and tie a knot at one end.

Look at the pattern and decide what "path" to take as you stitch. Take your needle to the back of the fabric. Bring the needle up and through (your first hole 1) to start stitching. Try to use as little thread as possible, the way Elizabethan stitchers did.

Follow the chart and backstitch along the solid lines. If you need to dou-

ble back, turn the fabric over and weave the needle back through the stitches. If you run out of thread, tie it off and start a new one.

To frame your project, measure its design area with a ruler. Cut a hole in the middle of the card stock that's a little bit bigger than the size of your design. Tape the fabric to the back of the card stock. Be sure that your design is centered in the hole.

Can you imagine the hours that embroiderers spent working on Elizabeth's magnificent gowns?

Gillyflower © Paula Kate Marmor, from the Blackwork Embroidery Archives

Lily © Paula Kate Marmor, from the Blackwork Embroidery Archives

in games of tickling Elizabeth, who was still dressed in her nightclothes.

These games, as innocent as Seymour made them seem, put Elizabeth into an awkward spot. Lots of people at Chelsea watched Seymour in action. Tongues wagged and gossip spread. Elizabeth, now 15, was a young woman. She understood that Seymour's attentions were inappropriate. Seymour's advances flattered her, but they frightened her as well.

Katherine became pregnant with Seymour's child, and she began to worry about the attention her husband paid to Elizabeth.

Without warning, Elizabeth left to live with another aristocratic family in mid-1548. With some space between them, and Seymour well away from the princess, Katherine and Elizabeth kept up their friendship. Then tragedy struck. Katherine died giving birth, leaving Seymour free to look for another wife.

He was handsome and fun, but Thomas Seymour proved to be a snake. Rumors spread that Seymour had asked Elizabeth to marry him. That news put Seymour in the bad graces of the Privy Council. Only a monarch—or the Privy Council, because Prince Edward was so young—could grant permission to marry Elizabeth.

And Seymour had made other enemies. His older brother, the lord protector, suspected that Seymour was plotting against him. The lord protector and the Privy Council ordered Seymour to be taken to the Tower of London. Seymour had few friends to plead his case, but the council pushed through a charge of treason. Seymour paid the price for betraying his country and was beheaded in March 1549.

Now it was Elizabeth's turn to worry about her reputation. Some powerful men felt that Kat Ashley, her governess, had not stepped in to protect Elizabeth when she lived with Katherine and Seymour. Kat had a loose tongue, and she had chatted about the prospect of Elizabeth marrying Seymour.

Kat paid for her gossip. She and another loyal servant were thrown into the Tower of London, where they were pressured to confess that Elizabeth had plotted treason with Seymour all along. Both prisoners, however, insisted that Elizabeth was innocent of any wrongdoing. Even so, embarrassing stories about Seymour and Elizabeth came to light.

The Privy Council ordered a knight and his wife to move into Elizabeth's home. The knight was to question Elizabeth about her dealings with Seymour. Elizabeth tried to protect her servants. She never spoke about all that had happened back when she lived in Thomas Seymour's home.

Time and distance had given Elizabeth a sharp picture of Seymour's true nature, as well as her own unschooled ways with men who

Thomas Seymour schemed to marry Princess Elizabeth.

✿ Munch on Marzipan

IT'S POSSIBLE that Queen Elizabeth tasted chocolate in a Spanish drink laced with sugar, cinnamon, and vanilla, but she never tasted a brownie or a chocolate bar. Elizabethans adored a confection called marchpane, today known as marzipan. Cooks stirred together ground almonds and water flavored with rose petals to make a sweet, stiff dough. Elizabeth had a sweet tooth and munched on marzipan. Did she think about the sacks of almonds and hours of grinding it took to make it?

Marizpan dough had lots of uses. Chefs created giant marzipan figures and set them out as decorations for feasts. Small marzipan figures shaped like fruits or animals were eaten like candy.

You can make marzipan by mixing equal parts of almond paste and powdered sugar. Egg whites hold everything together.

You'll Need

- ✿ Apron
- ✿ Cutting board or cookie sheet
- ✿ Almond paste (it comes in cans or tubes)
- ✿ Mixing bowl
- ✿ Powdered sugar
- ✿ Small fork
- ✿ Egg whites—fresh or packaged (some people prefer not to eat uncooked eggs—you can find dried egg whites in the grocery store)
- ✿ Small bowls
- ✿ Food coloring
- ✿ Toothpick

Put on an apron and set out a cutting board or cookie sheet as your work space. Making marzipan can get messy—especially when you mix in the food coloring!

Remove the almond paste from the can and put it in the mixing bowl. Add an equal amount of powdered sugar. You can use a bit more or less, depending on how sweet you want it to be. Use a fork and your hands to blend the almond paste and sugar together. Mix it well.

Now add just enough egg whites to make the dough pull together so you can mold it like clay. It will feel like stiff cookie dough. At this point, you can wrap the dough in plastic wrap and store in the freezer until you are ready to use it, or move on to the coloring step.

Divide the marzipan into sections and place into small bowls. Use food coloring a drop at a time to color the dough. Think about the color wheel and make lots of colors.

To make fruits and vegetables, pull off tiny bits of marzipan and shape with your fingers. Use a small fork or toothpick to make dents or dots. Add whole cloves for stems. Arrange your fruits and veggies on a pretty plate.

You can freeze your marzipan creations to eat later.

Fruits and veggies are just two ways you can mold marzipan. Next time, try your hand at making animals, fish, birds, and buildings.

held power. Elizabeth made up her mind to learn from her mistakes, and she was careful to admit nothing. But in the Tower of London, Kat Ashley had made a confession.

Now the knight laid out a copy of Kat's confession and its nasty stories in front of her. In a garden the year before, Kat and Katherine Parr had seen Elizabeth encircled in Seymour's arms. But Elizabeth refused to admit any guilt. She wrote a letter to the lord protector arguing Kat's innocence, and thereby, her own:

> *. . . paraventure your Lordeship and the rest of the Counsel wil thinke that I favor her ivel doinge for whome I shal speake for, wiche is for Kateryn Aschiley [Kat Ashley], that it wolde please your grace and the rest of the Counsel to be good unto her. . . . First, bicause that she hathe bene with me a longe time, and manye years, and hathe taken great labor, and paine in brinkinge of me up in lerninge and honestie, and therfore I ough of very dewtye speke for her, for Saint Gregorie sayeth that we ar more bounde to them that bringeth us up wel than to our parents, for our parents do that wiche is natural for them, that is bringeth us into this Worlde; but our brinkers up ar a cause to make us live wel in it. The seconde is bicause I think that whatsoever she hathe done in my Lord Admirals matter as concerninge the marijnge of*

me, she dide it bicause knowinge him to be one of the Counsel, . . . for I have ahrde her manye times say that she wolde never have me mary in any place without your Graces and the Counsels consente. The thirde cause is bicause that it shal and doth make men thinke that I am not clere of the dide myselfe, but that it is pardoned in me bicause of my youthe, bicause that she I loved so wel is in suche a place.

In the end, the Privy Council could find no evidence of treason and no fault with Elizabeth other than simple foolishness. She had passed her first true test. Intelligent she was, and now the princess had learned that she could trust no one.

Elizabeth was starting to realize that she was a prize. Like other highborn ladies of her day, she would have little choice about a husband. As a princess, she would be betrothed—married off—to a highborn aristocrat, perhaps a king or prince.

When she wed, powerful men would bargain over how much land and money she would bring to the marriage as a gift to her husband. And when she came to the marriage, it would be to give birth to sons to carry on her husband's name. If her husband actually loved her, it would be a stroke of luck.

AN IMPRISONED PRINCESS

3

ONCE AGAIN in the Privy Council's favor, Elizabeth often visited her brother Edward at court. Edward was still too young to rule, and England had a new lord protector, John Dudley, the duke of Northumberland. The duke wormed his way into Edward's good graces and, with great skill, persuaded Edward to approve every move he made.

Edward VI, the boy king, was never to rule England as a man. In the winter of 1553, Edward grew sick with a horrible cough. By springtime it was plain that he suffered from tuberculosis, a disease of the lungs. With every wheeze from his lungs and every pound he lost, Edward moved closer to his end. The duke of Northumberland, a passionate Protestant, dreaded the future. With Edward's final breath, his Catholic half sister Mary would become queen.

Men were deceivers ever,
One foot in sea,
  and one on shore,
To one thing constant never.

—William Shakespeare,
Much Ado About Nothing

King Edward VI, Elizabeth's younger brother, died at age 16.

Northumberland launched a plot to keep power in Edward's family. The duke coaxed the young king into replacing Henry VIII's will with a new one. Edward's new will dropped Mary and Elizabeth Tudor from the line of royal succession.

Northumberland supplied the perfect substitute, a Tudor relative named Lady Jane Grey, who was Mary's and Elizabeth's cousin. Jane's heartless parents joined in Northumberland's plot. Together, they forced Jane to marry Northumberland's son, Guildford Dudley. The luckless Jane, just 15 years old, had no say in the plot.

On July 8, 1553, King Edward VI died, and two days later Lady Jane Grey was proclaimed queen. But Mary Tudor refused to step aside for her cousin, and she gathered supporters into an army. Most of England followed the wishes of Henry VIII and sided with Mary.

Within days, Northumberland's plot unraveled. Mary's supporters declared victory and marched with her to London. The duke, his son, and Lady Jane Grey were thrown into the Tower of London. In time, all three lost their heads.

Mary Tudor, Queen of England

ORDERS REACHED Elizabeth that she was to join Mary, England's new queen, on her procession to claim England's throne. Mounted on horseback, with Mary in the lead, the two sisters rode into London. Crowds cheered and church bells rang. As with the rise of any new monarch, hopes ran high for England's future.

Daughters of the same father, Mary and Elizabeth looked completely different. The dark-haired Mary was 37, once attractive but now an old woman in many people's eyes. Elizabeth, at 20, appeared young and shining. Her father's reddish hair streamed down her back, giving her the look of a Tudor.

But the physical contrast was just one of their differences. Elizabeth symbolized a threat to Mary's throne. Elizabeth, as a Protestant, would have the backing of England's powerful Protestant nobles if she became queen.

Eventually, Mary's reign brought trouble to England. Mary, a faithful Catholic, stayed true to the ideals taught by her church. Soon after she arrived in London, she brought back the Catholic Church as England's state religion.

Unlike her father and brother, Mary bowed to the pope in Rome as the head of England's church. Mary installed Catholic bishops in England's cathedrals, and Protestant bishops found themselves imprisoned as traitors to the "true faith" of Catholics. Churches dropped the Anglican service of worship. Once again, the Catholic mass was said in churches across the land.

Elizabeth pretended to convert to the Catholic faith. She attended mass at the royal court as Mary insisted. Still, Mary doubted that Elizabeth had any true change of heart in matters of faith. Elizabeth, wary of the eyes that followed her at court, asked Mary for permission to leave the queen's court to live in the countryside.

Mary granted Elizabeth her wish, but for the next five years, Elizabeth had to watch her ways and choose her words with care. As William Shakespeare wrote later, "walls have ears," and Queen Mary's spies listened for proof that Elizabeth was a Protestant.

Matters grew more complicated when Mary looked for a husband. The choice was tricky, because any man who married the queen would become England's king. Of course, Mary would think only of marrying another Catholic, a man who would father a son to follow her and her Catholic ways.

A Spanish ambassador came to Mary's royal court and suggested that the queen should marry

LEFT: An innocent pawn in a family plot to gain England's throne, Lady Jane Grey met her death in the Tower of London.
RIGHT: Lady Jane Grey and Elizabeth's mother, Queen Anne Boleyn, are buried under the floor of a chapel in the Tower of London.

Spain's future king, Prince Philip. Though he was 10 years younger than Mary, Philip seemed to be the perfect choice. A strong Catholic, he was the head of a rich, powerful nation. Mary's advisers hoped that Philip could provide the Catholic son Mary hoped for. Once and for all, the marriage would seal the bonds between tiny England and mighty Spain.

Much Suspected, Nothing Proved

MARY MARRIED Philip and made him king of England. In the streets, Englishmen and women complained. The queen had brought a foreigner to rule their county—from Spain, no less! Mary had been queen only a few months when Protestant nobles started plotting to replace her with Elizabeth. Their leader, Sir Thomas Wyatt, laid out his plans.

Wyatt's small army marched for London in February 1555. However, the people of London stayed true to the laws that made Mary their rightful queen. They fought back against Wyatt's troops at the city gates, and Wyatt surrendered. Several other nobles, Wyatt's partners, were hunted, captured, and charged with treason against the Queen's Majesty.

Mary's men turned over every rock to investigate Wyatt's plan and asked the questions on everyone's mind: What part did Elizabeth have

in the plot? Was she guilty of treason? Mary and her Privy Council could not be sure, so they ordered Elizabeth to London to answer their questions. It didn't matter that Elizabeth was very ill.

Pale and sick from a kidney infection, Elizabeth had no choice except to obey the order. Even so, she managed to polish her image as she made her way to Mary's court.

England's people liked to see their rulers in person. A smart king—or princess—could turn a simple journey into a pageant. Elizabeth issued her orders. Instead of riding on horseback in a look of power, she returned to court on a litter, a covered stretcher carried by men and horses. The curtains of her litter were pulled back so that onlookers could see her, sick as she was. Cleverly, she dressed in white, the color of a pure soul.

However, Mary's lead councillor, a Catholic bishop named Stephen Gardiner, convinced the queen that Elizabeth was up to no good. Elizabeth was at court only three weeks when the strong-minded bishop had his way, and Mary's council ordered Elizabeth to the Tower of London. On March 15, she was escorted to a barge on the Thames River. On that rainy day, Elizabeth entered the Tower in the same way her mother had, through Traitors' Gate.

Elizabeth knew she must make the best of a bad situation. She entered prison with all the

England's Queen Mary Tudor and her husband, King Philip of Spain.

✿ Fly Your Banner

IN THE 1500s, symbols mattered. England flew banners with the red cross of St. George on a white background. The Irish were fond of displaying harps. In Scotland, the white cross of St. Andrew was popular. The Scottish monarchy had another symbol: the rampant lion standing on his back legs.

With some paper, fabric, tissue paper, and glue, you can make a Scottish banner using a modern technique: mixed media.

You'll Need

- ✿ Large piece of paper and pencil
- ✿ Scissors
- ✿ Thin permanent marker
- ✿ Piece of muslin fabric, 18 inches wide by 30 inches long
- ✿ Large piece of slick paper (butcher paper or waxed paper)
- ✿ Masking tape
- ✿ Variety of colored tissue paper
- ✿ White craft glue
- ✿ Paintbrush
- ✿ Toothpick
- ✿ Thin dowel rod
- ✿ Yarn

On a sheet of paper, enlarge the pattern on the next page to draw a full-sized outline of the lion. On the grid, one square equals one inch. Cut out the paper pattern. Then use a permanent marker to trace the lion onto the muslin. Add details such as the lion's eye, mane, hip, and elbow.

Now lay the muslin on the slick paper with the slick side up. Hold it in place with a few pieces of masking tape.

Cut out or tear pieces of tissue paper. Play around with the colors to see how to color your lion.

Mix craft glue with water in a small bowl until it's thin and watery. Paint an area of the lion with the glue. While the glue is still wet, place a piece of tissue paper over the area and apply more of the mixture on top of the paper until it's damp, but not soaked through.

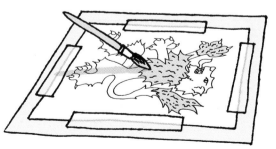

Use the toothpick to help push the paper into smaller areas. The paper might crumple into a wet mass, but that's OK. Work on one area at a time. From time to time, step back to look at your lion. Do you like the 3-D effect?

When you have finished, set your banner aside to dry thoroughly. Once it's dry, peel the muslin away from the slick paper backing.

To hang your banner, make a 1½-inch fold along the top. Run a strip of glue along the folded-back edge. Let dry.

Place the dowel rod through the top of the banner and hang with yarn, as shown. You are now ready to fly your banner!

❀ Fly Your Banner (continued)

dignity of a Tudor princess. Once she alighted from the boat, Elizabeth sat down in the rain and refused to stand up. No one tried to move her.

When she was sure her jailers understood that they were dealing with a strong-willed princess, Elizabeth stood up. Holding herself straight, she strode through the Tower's cold stone walls.

Mary's councillors tried to wear Elizabeth out with long hours of questioning about Wyatt's plot, but they dared not touch the princess. But Wyatt and his fellow conspirators were not so lucky. Nothing could stop Mary's men from torturing them—"marvelously tossed and examined," a chronicler wrote. Yet Mary's councillors could never link Elizabeth to the plan.

For his part, Wyatt mounted the executioner's scaffold at Tower Hill on April 11, where he died in front of every man and woman who came to gawk. Before he was beheaded, Wyatt proclaimed that Princess Elizabeth had done no wrong. Wyatt's body was cut into pieces and "his quarters were set up in divers [diverse] places and his head on the gallows at Hay Hill near Hyde Park." Such was the warning to those who dared to plot against the queen.

Without any evidence linking her to the plot, there was no good reason to keep Elizabeth in the Tower. In mid-May, Elizabeth left, not by Traitors' Gate but through the Tower's main entrance. She journeyed to a new home at Woodstock to live under house arrest.

The Tragedy of Mary Tudor

MARY TUDOR'S councillors and churchmen kept hunting for Protestants. Mary felt that she was doing a godly thing. In her heart of hearts, she believed that Protestants were heretics—traitors to God and to the Catholic Church that she loved. And for that, the Church said, they must die.

Once a Church court declared a person guilty, the government carried out the punishment. In Mary Tudor's day, this meant death by burning at the stake. Only fire could cleanse the soul of a heretic.

All over England, Protestants met their deaths by fire. Bishops and priests from the Church of England, as well as ordinary women and men, were executed. Even a few children died. A poet captured England's distress over these Protestant martyrs:

With furious force of sword and fire;
When man and wife were put to death:
We wished for our Queen Elizabeth.

Queen Mary prayed that she would give birth to a son. But her wish never came. Twice the

ABOVE: The prisoner Elizabeth was said to have scratched words in the wall. They said: *Much suspected by me, Nothing proved can be.*
LEFT: Traitors' Gate didn't get its name until long after Princess Elizabeth lived.

queen thought she was expecting a child, even to the point of looking pregnant. But Mary's body played cruel tricks on her. Both times, these "pregnancies" turned out to be false.

In the meantime, Philip's father died, so he left Mary and returned to Spain to rule as king. Philip had never loved Mary, though she loved him deeply. When the hoped-for child never appeared, Philip did not bother to come back to his wife.

Philip thought of Mary and Elizabeth Tudor as pieces on a game board. Philip believed that if Mary died, it would be in Spain's best interest for Elizabeth to follow her as queen. Otherwise, France would promote its choice, Mary, Queen of Scots, who was half French.

ABOVE: Burning at the stake was punishment for heretics during Mary Tudor's reign

RIGHT: The forbidding Tower of London was the setting for many scenes in the Tudors' lives.

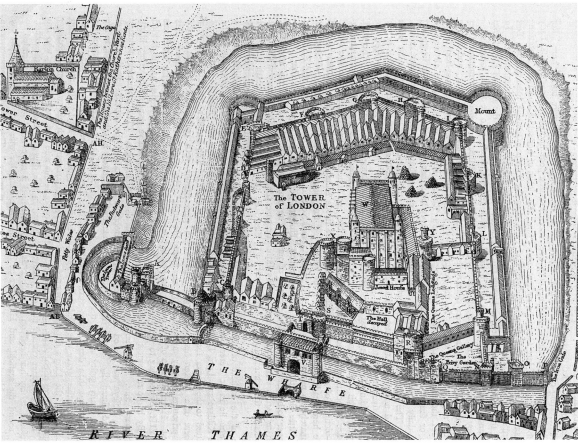

✿ Play Nine Men's Morris

ELIZABETHANS LOVED to play all kinds of games. There were Elizabethan forms of poker called primero as well as games with playing pieces similar to today's chess, backgammon, and checkers.

Nine Men's Morris was a well-known game in Elizabeth's day. It's a bit like a mixture of checkers and tic-tac-toe, except that the game starts as players put their pieces on the board.

Make your own game board for Nine Men's Morris. Then pick a partner and read up on the rules. They are simple to learn. Enjoy the fun!

You'll Need
- ✿ Pencil
- ✿ Ruler
- ✿ Piece of heavy cardboard
- ✿ Black permanent marker
- ✿ 9 pennies
- ✿ 9 dimes

Elizabethan men playing the game of primero.

Use a pencil and ruler to help you copy the game board on this page onto the cardboard. Enlarge it if you wish. Check your work to make sure it's an exact copy of the original. Then, use the ruler to help you darken the lines with a permanent marker.

Are you ready to play? Here are the rules for Nine Men's Morris:

Object of the Game: To remove all but two of your opponent's pieces from the board *or* block your opponent from making any moves.

The Basic Strategy: A player makes a "mill" by lining up three pieces in a horizontal or vertical row along a dark line. Every time a mill is made, that player removes one of the opponent's pieces from the board. A new mill is made even when the same piece is moved in and out of a mill that's already on the board.

Starting the Game: Play begins by placing the pieces on the board. Player 1 uses nine pennies, and Player 2 uses nine dimes. Toss a coin to see who starts first. The winner of the toss places one piece on any spot on the board. The other player follows, taking turns, until all pieces are on the board. Note: A player may make a mill when placing pieces on the board and remove an opponent's piece. Of course, the other player may place a piece to block it.

Play: Once all pieces are placed, players take turns moving pieces around the board. Each player moves

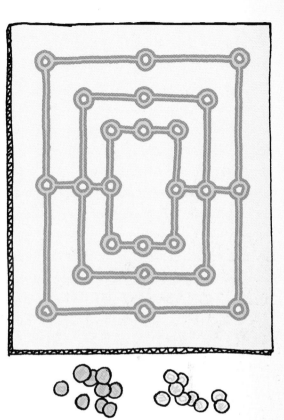

one piece at a time, one space at a time, always trying to make a mill or block the opponent from making one.

Declaring a Winner: The game ends when one player has just two pieces left, or if a player is blocked in and has no more moves to make. The player with more than two pieces, or who blocks the opponent, is the winner.

As you play the game, you will start to understand the strategy behind it.

Names for All and Titles for Some

"WHAT'S IN a name?" asked Romeo in Will Shakespeare's play *Romeo and Juliet*. In Queen Elizabeth's times, a name meant everything. People had two—their given name and their family's name.

For ordinary folk born on farms or in towns, that was it. But if a boy or girl were lucky enough to be born in England's upper classes, the game of names became more complicated. These children held titles that identified their special place in society. Babies born into Elizabeth's immediate family, the Tudors, were royal children and bore the title of Prince or Princess.

Just beneath the tiny group of royals stood England's noble families. The male heads of these families were called peers, and there were about 60 peers when Elizabeth ruled England. Peers were divided by their rank. Dukes topped the list of peers:

DUKE (a duke's wife held the courtesy title duchess)

MARQUIS (wife's courtesy title: marchioness)

EARL (wife's courtesy title: countess)

VISCOUNT (wife's courtesy title: viscountess)

BARON (wife's courtesy title: baroness)

A male peer was called My Lord, and his wife was addressed as My Lady. Elizabeth also awarded knighthoods to deserving men. A knight and his wife were called Sir and Lady. However, they did not rank as nobles.

Elizabeth gave titles to her courtiers as she saw fit, but she kept the ranks of nobles small so she could control them. Just one duke lived when Elizabeth was queen, and after he was beheaded for treason, Elizabeth did not give his title to anyone else.

Once a man earned a title, it was his to keep and pass on to his oldest son after he died. Often titles came with large tracts of land with buildings and farms, and many nobles lived grandly.

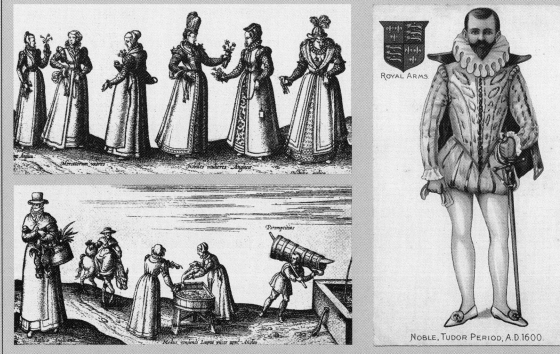

LEFT: Well-off Elizabethan women dressed far more grandly than peasants.
RIGHT: This antique postcard shows how Elizabethan noblemen dressed.

To Philip, that possibility was unthinkable—Spain and France hated each other.

Elizabeth watched and waited quietly. Another plot to overthrow Mary came to light, but again Elizabeth stayed away from its sticky web of lies and tricks. As always, she continued to swear her loyalty to her older sister.

Mary's second false pregnancy turned out to be a fatal illness. By the fall of 1558 it was clear that she was dying. With no child to inherit her throne, Mary accepted reality. She agreed that Elizabeth, though a hated Protestant, would succeed her as England's next queen.

On November 17, 1558, priests and monks circled Mary's deathbed. She died firm in her belief that she had done God's work in persecuting heretics. Her body dressed in nun's clothing, she was buried among other kings and queens in Westminster Abbey, England's royal church. But no one bothered to put a marker on Mary's grave.

She died not knowing that history would call her Bloody Mary, on whose shoulders rested the deaths of 300 people.

✿ Scent Your Home with a Pomander

ELIZABETHANS ENJOYED wearing pretty clothes, but there was a price to pay. Their homes crawled with vermin, such as rats and fleas, sure to find their way into the chests and wardrobes where they stored their clothes. Moths left tiny holes in the wool of costly garments.

Folks prized scented pomanders (POM-ander) to bring good smells inside. These were made with all kinds of flowers and spices such as cloves and cinnamon.

Bring some Elizabethan spice into your life by making pomanders.

You'll Need
- ✿ Spices to mix, such as cinnamon, nutmeg, ginger, and/or cloves
- ✿ Spoon
- ✿ Shallow bowl
- ✿ Plastic work surface
- ✿ Large container of whole cloves
- ✿ Oranges, lemons, and limes
- ✿ Pushpin or small nail
- ✿ Flat container
- ✿ Ribbon

First, mix 2 teaspoons of each spice in a small flat bowl. Set aside.

Protect your table with the plastic mat. Start making pomanders by pushing the sharp ends of whole cloves into the skin of the fruit. You might need to use the pushpin first to make the process easier. If you wish, create a pattern with the cloves. Your imagination is the limit!

When you like the look of your pomander, roll it in the spice mixture and set it in a flat container. As you fill the box with pomanders, be sure they don't touch each other.

Allow the pomanders to dry for several weeks in a warm, dry place away from light. They will start to shrivel up and harden—but give them a sniff. Don't they smell nice?

Fill a pretty bowl with your pomanders. Or, tie them with some ribbon and hang them in your closet. They will last for many months.

QUEEN, PRINCE, AND PLAYER

4

Men at some time are masters of their fates

—William Shakespeare, *Julius Caesar*

QUEEN MARY was dead, and there wasn't a moment to lose. Courtiers from London mounted horses and rode west to Hatfield. There was a new queen waiting.

The messengers galloped across Hatfield's grounds to the house, but Elizabeth wasn't inside. She had gone outdoors for some air—Elizabeth always liked to take walks in a garden—and the horsemen found her seated on a bench under an oak tree. They bowed and told Elizabeth the news.

The Queen was dead. Long live the Queen!

Elizabeth listened and then knelt on the ground. She stayed quiet for a few moments, thinking about what to say. Then she answered the group in Latin, and they did not forget her words. "This is the doing of the Lord," she said, "and it is marvelous in our eyes."

William Cecil and Son

ELIZABETH PLANNED to rule England in a strategic way to protect herself and her monarchy. Before she entered London to be crowned, she assembled a group of men to serve as advisers on her Privy Council. Among them was Sir William Cecil, from a family well known to Tudor kings and queens.

The Cecils did not arise from England's noble families but from its middle-class townspeople. Smart and hardworking, three generations of Cecils had served the Tudors. William Cecil's grandfather and father had chosen wives from good families, and each generation rose a bit higher in English society.

Elizabeth trusted Cecil as much as she cared to trust anyone. He was to serve as her closest adviser for 40 years. When he came to Elizabeth's court, Cecil brought along his son Robert, a "hunchback" with a crooked spine. The queen, who had pet names for her favorites, took a liking to the little boy and nicknamed him Frog. He stayed loyal to her throughout his life and grew up to replace his father as Elizabeth's trusted adviser.

The Date Is Set

ELIZABETH'S PRIVY Council met to make a key decision: the date for her coronation. The exact date mattered deeply. All agreed that in order to give the new queen the best possible start, the stars in the sky must line up in just the right way. The Privy Council consulted an expert, an astrologer named John Dee. They needed him to read Elizabeth's horoscope to find the best day for Elizabeth's coronation.

In Elizabeth's day, people thought that the motion of planets and stars shaped one's destiny. Astrologers like Dee traced the path of the sun, moon, planets, and stars in order to predict the future. Dee consulted his charts of the night sky and declared that Elizabeth's lucky day would be in mid-January.

Elizabeth left Hatfield for London to prepare for her coronation. People jammed the streets to greet her. Ready to play the role of queen, Elizabeth shed the plain clothes she had worn as a princess. Now she dressed in purple velvet to meet her adoring subjects. She stopped to speak with ordinary folk, and they greeted her with jolly shouts.

All of London looked forward to coronation day. Following custom, Elizabeth left Whitehall Palace and boarded a royal barge flying the monarch's flag to carry her down the Thames River to the Tower of London. Once Elizabeth's prison, the Tower now bustled with activity as hundreds of people, from lords and bishops to serving men and maids, prepared for the grand event.

William Cecil, Queen Elizabeth's closest adviser. Elizabeth made Cecil a noble with the title Lord Burghley. © istockphoto/nicoolay

CAST OF CHARACTERS: *William Shakespeare*

EVERY SCHOOLGIRL or boy who studies English, no matter where on earth they live, has read works written by William Shakespeare. Modern audiences can see their own lives mirrored in Shakespeare's plays and poems although they are more than 400 years old. However, many details about Shakespeare's own life are dim.

William Shakespeare.

Born in Stratford in 1564, Will Shakespeare grew up with Elizabeth as his queen. No one can say for sure, but it's likely that young Will attended grammar school in the thriving town. If so, he would have studied with other boys whose fathers made good livings and wanted their sons to have the advantages that an education would offer.

As a youth, Will had an unusual gift for understanding human nature, a talent that usually develops in much older people. He kept his sharp eyes and keen mind alert to the goings-on among the people of Stratford. To Will Shakespeare, the life of every man and woman was a play that unfolded as the sun rose and set each day.

At 18, Shakespeare became involved with an older woman named Anne Hathaway. Soon after they married, their first daughter was born, followed by twins, a boy and a girl. Like many fathers in his day, Will Shakespeare experienced his own tragedy when his son died at age 11. No record tells us how Shakespeare dealt with his loss.

Life in Stratford proved to be too small a stage for the likes of Will Shakespeare. In the early 1590s, he left his wife and daughters and moved to London, where he joined a company of actors and began to write plays. By 1592, he had made a splash in London, although a well-known playwright there made fun of his "Shake-scenes" and laughed at Will for not going to a university.

But Will Shakespeare did not need a university education to understand the ways of the human heart and mind. He left proof of that in his plays and poems.

Do you recognize their names? Here are a few:

Romeo and Juliet	*Julius Caesar*
Macbeth	*Hamlet*
A Midsummer	*Twelfth Night*
Night's Dream	*Richard III*
King Lear	

Shakespeare is not buried among other great poets in Westminster Abbey. After he died, no one dared move his body from the graveyard in Stratford. As his epitaph, Shakespeare had written:

good frend for jesus sake forbeare [do not] *to digg the dust encloased heare.*
blest be ye [the] *man yt* [that] *spares thes stones and*
curst be he yt moves my bones

Elizabeth Reads the Stars

THE ASTROLOGER John Dee set the date for Elizabeth's coronation based on her birth date of September 7, 1533. Elizabeth believed her life was ruled according to the stars, by the astrological sign of Leo, the Lion.

The constellation Leo is one sign of the zodiac, a series of constellations that rotates, relative to the sun, like a giant wheel overhead. It takes one full year for the wheel to turn as it follows the ecliptic, the path of the sun as it appears to people on earth. Elizabethans didn't know that the earth rotates and revolves around the sun. They assumed that the sun, moon, and stars circled the earth.

Astrology arose among ancient peoples in the Middle East and Asia. Astrologers divided the zodiac into 12 sections and assigned a constellation to each. The sun was said to be "in" a constellation when the constellation sat high in the sky at midday and sunlight blocked it from view. Elizabeth could not see Leo on her birthday in September, but Leo was visible at night six months later in March.

Modern astronomers—scientists who study stars—still use constellations to help them map the stars. They also use telescopes that

A clock shows the conventional zodiac.
© iStockphoto/Baloncici

Elizabethans never had to study the sky, even during daylight. Now they observe the sun passing through Leo about one month later than it did in ancient times.

Why? Over time, earth's position relative to the zodiac has changed, when compared to the position of the sun. To a current observer on earth, the zodiac has moved. However, astrologers today use the same dates for the zodiac that the Elizabethans did.

Astrological Signs and the Zodiac

ASTROLOGICAL "SUN" SIGNS	ZODIAC DATES
Pisces "The Fishes"	February 19–March 20
Aries "The Ram"	March 21–April 19
Taurus "The Bull"	April 20–May 20
Gemini "The Twins"	May 21–June 20
Cancer "The Crab"	June 21–July 22
Leo "The Lion"	July 23–August 22
Virgo "The Maiden"	August 23–September 22
Libra "The Lyre"	September 23–October 22
Scorpius "The Scorpion"	October 23–November 21
Sagittarius "The Archer"	November 22–December 21
Capricornus "The Sea Goat"	December 22–January 19
Aquarius "The Water Carrier"	January 20–February 18

(NOTE: Taurus, Gemini, Leo, and Scorpius are easy to see at night in a big city even with light pollution. Aries, Virgo, Sagittarius, and Capricornus are harder to find. Pisces, Cancer, Libra, and Aquarius are very faint and are best viewed far away from towns.)

On the afternoon before the Sunday coronation, a thousand men rallied to escort the princess through the Tower's double walls and onto London's streets. Elizabeth rode on a chariot pulled by mules. Everything—mules, chariot, and the princess herself—was adorned in gold.

People swarmed the procession and gave Elizabeth small gifts. One poor woman handed Elizabeth a branch of rosemary, a fragrant herb. Both the giver and the receiver knew its power. Rosemary symbolized memory and faithfulness, the woman's hopes for a bright future under her new queen.

Along the parade route, Elizabeth viewed a series of five pageants staged in her honor. Each pageant displayed a scene from the Bible or other famous event from history. As Elizabeth paused to view each pageant, she, and everyone around her, understood that it taught a lesson.

In the first pageant, actors represented her Tudor ancestors, including her disgraced mother, Anne Boleyn. In another, eight children symbolized the eight beatitudes—a list of the groups of people who have God's blessing—that Jesus delivered in his Sermon on the Mount. Like Jesus, the children reminded Elizabeth to be pure in heart, meek, merciful, and a peacemaker. As queen, Elizabeth needed to care for the poor, the sad, the hungry, and the persecuted.

Elizabeth's chariot moved on to the fourth pageant, which contrasted Mary Tudor's bleak reign with people's hopes for Elizabeth. The scene showed two hills, one each for Mary and Elizabeth, with a cave in between. On Mary's hill stood a boy dressed in black beside a dead tree. On Elizabeth's grassy green hill stood a leafy tree and a boy wearing bright colors.

As Elizabeth watched, two figures came from the cave to greet her. One was an old man dressed as "Time" and the other, his daughter "Truth." With God's blessing, they said, Time and Truth promised to carry Elizabeth through a good and just reign.

Two Crowns for a Queen

ON THE frosty morning of January 15, 1559, Elizabeth entered Westminster Abbey to be crowned queen. The lords and ladies of England, together with Elizabeth's councillors and bishops, crowded into the magnificent church to watch the spectacle. Like so many kings before her, Elizabeth took a seat on the coronation chair, a carved wooden chair used to crown England's heads of state for hundreds of years.

Elizabeth was 25 and not considered young, but she wore her hair long like any unmarried woman. With great dignity, she listened to the proclamations that made her queen. A bishop

❀ Stargaze and Observe the Zodiac

SUPERSTITIOUS ELIZABETHANS practiced astrology and believed that the positions of the sun, moon, and planets predicted the future. Today we know that is false. But Elizabethan astrologists also were doing science when they studied the night sky, observing and tracking celestial bodies. Much later in the 1600s, scholars called this work astronomy.

Think like an Elizabethan *and* a scientist. Look for constellations that follow the ecliptic in the night sky.

You'll Need

- ❀ 3 large paper plates
- ❀ Scissors
- ❀ Markers
- ❀ Pencil
- ❀ Zodiac from chart on page 42
- ❀ Nail or thick pin
- ❀ Paper fastener
- ❀ Flashlight

Cut the rim off a large paper plate to form a circle. This plate will represent night and day based on the position of the sun. On the edge of the plate, draw a picture of the sun and the labels Noon (next to the sun), Sunset, Midnight, and Sunrise as shown. Then shade the bottom half, opposite the sun.

Cut a second circle from another plate, about 2 inches smaller in diameter than the first. This plate

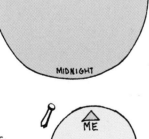

will represent the earth as it rotates. Draw a small triangle near the edge and label it Me.

Turn a third large paper plate upside down. Use the pencil to divide it into 12 equal pie-shaped sections. Using the zodiac chart, moving *counterclockwise*, label each section on the rim of the plate with each constellation and the dates it appears in the night sky. This plate will show the constellations that follow the ecliptic across the sky.

Use a nail to punch a hole in the center of each circle. Center the holes of each plate with the largest plate (constellations) on the bottom, the medium plate (sun) in the middle, and the smallest plate (earth) on top. Join all three plates using the paper fastener.

Now it's time to use your celestial wheel. Start by turning the middle sun dial to the current date on the outer wheel (this will only be approximate). While holding the sun and constellation wheels in place, turn the small earth wheel to Sunset. What constellation will be over your head at sunset tonight? Turn the earth wheel

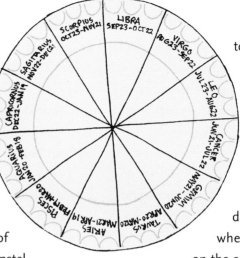

to Midnight. What constellation is overhead now?

Your celestial wheel can be used to find the time when your zodiac sign will be directly overhead. First, make sure the sun is turned to the current date. Holding the other two wheels in place, turn the Me on the earth wheel to point at your zodiac sign. Is it overhead at night, or during the day? Can you estimate the approximate time that it's overhead?

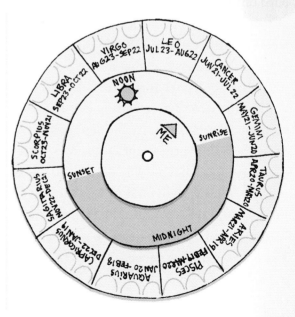

anointed her head with oil, a sign that she was God's chosen one. Then she withdrew behind a curtain to change her clothes. Always fussy about the way things smelled, she was heard to complain that the oil was old and rancid.

Nonetheless, when she emerged, Elizabeth the princess had transformed into Her Majesty the Queen. She wore a gold mantle and underneath, a robe of purple velvet, the color of royalty. As trumpets blew, a bishop slipped a ring onto her finger to symbolize Elizabeth's "marriage" to the people of England. She would not remove it until just before she died.

Then came the climax, as England's queen received her most important symbols of power: not one, but two crowns. The first, St. Edward's Crown, weighed only two pounds. The second, the Imperial Crown, weighed seven pounds, and Elizabeth wore it for only a few moments before exchanging it for the lighter one.

The bishops carried on with the rest of the religious ceremony and celebrated the Catholic mass. For the first time in years, people in the congregation heard part of the service spoken not in Latin but in English. This quiet change

This coronation portrait of Elizabeth I shows how Elizabeth looked that day. Her robe is embroidered with her family flower, the Tudor Rose, and trimmed in ermine, the fur only royals could wear. She holds a scepter and orb, symbols of royal power.

signaled that Elizabeth would return England to the Protestant church.

The new queen's court moved the celebration to nearby Westminster Hall for her coronation dinner. During the party, a knight, fully armored and astride his charger, rode into the banqueting hall. It was the queen's champion, Sir Edward Dymoke. The crowd hushed as the knight removed his gauntlet, a heavy glove, and hurled it on the floor.

Everyone understood the meaning of throwing down the gauntlet. Let anyone challenge his queen, the knight declared, and he would fight to defend her right to sit on England's throne. In time, Elizabeth's knights would meet that challenge.

A Queen in a Man's Kingdom

ELIZABETH MIGHT be England's rightful queen, but from the start, she had to prove herself. She was a woman in a world ruled by men. In her time, everyone believed women were born weak in both body and mind. They weren't made of sturdy stuff as men were. The Church said so.

Priests and ministers eyed Elizabeth warily. Some ministers spoke openly against the idea of a queen ruling England. Churchmen—Protestant and Catholic—compared women to the Bible character Eve and taught that women were the cause of sin. Against the orders of God himself, Eve had tempted Adam to eat an apple he picked from the Tree of Knowledge in the Garden of Eden. The Church taught that Eve was a sinner, along with her daughters for generations to come.

One minister roared that "God hath revealed to some in this our age that it is more than a monster in nature that a woman should reign

The Dymoke family served as the ceremonial champions to England's kings and queens for centuries. Royal College of Arms

Queen Elizabeth understood the meaning of this German woodcut. It shows an angel driving Adam and Eve out of the Garden of Eden.

✿ Fluff Up a Ruff

IN ELIZABETHAN England, both men and women sported ruffs, which came into fashion when Edward VI sat on the throne. At first, ruffs were rather small, decorative touches to a removable collar that protected the wearer's clothes. But as England grew in glory during the years of Elizabeth, ruffs swelled into large, round rolls. One reason that giant ruffs came into fashion was that they could be shaped with long irons heated in a fire and stiffened with starch, a new product in the late 1500s.

A Puritan minister complained that ruffs were "an invention of the devil... smeared and starched in the devils liquore." Queen Elizabeth, however, adored big ruffs and paid no attention to Puritan warnings.

You can make a ruff that will stand up all by itself. All you need are a few simple tools and some wire-edge ribbon.

Adult supervision required

YOU'LL NEED
- ✿ 18 feet of wire-edge craft ribbon, 1¾ inches wide (often sold on 9-foot spools, white or silver gauzy ribbon works best)
- ✿ Tape measure
- ✿ Heavy, slippery thread, such as fishing line, kite string, or dental floss
- ✿ Scissors
- ✿ Large, sharp sewing needle with a big eye
- ✿ Partner
- ✿ Craft glue
- ✿ 2 Velcro fasteners

Unroll the ribbon from each spool. Fold two inches of the ribbon at each end back over itself. Press the folds with your fingers.

Measure out a piece of heavy thread, 10 feet long. Cut the thread and insert one end through the eye of the needle. Then double the thread by matching the ends. Tie the ends together with a large knot. You will have a 5-foot-long piece of thread.

Pick up the end of one piece of ribbon and gather it into loose folds, as shown below. *Do not press the folds.* Keep gathering folds until you have about 12 inches of gathered ribbon.

Center the point of the needle at one end of the ribbon. Push the needle through three folds of the ribbon, as shown. Pull the thread through the folds, leaving a 12-inch tail.

Now make another knot right up against the ribbon. This will "lock" the ribbon in place to keep it from sliding back.

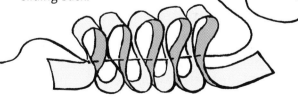

Continue sewing through the center of each group of folds.

Repeat the process of gathering the ribbon and sewing through it. Are you starting to see your ruff appear? When you reach the end of the ribbon, attach the folded-in edge to the second piece of ribbon following the diagram below.

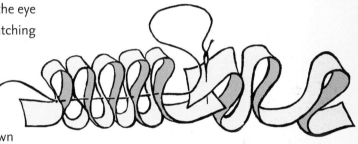

Continue to gather and sew the ribbon until you reach the end. Cut off the thread with the needle and tie a sturdy knot at the end of the thread. You should have extra thread left.

Ask your partner to place the ruff around your neck. Your partner can adjust the ruff by sliding it along the thread so it fits snug and smooth. When your ruff looks right, knot the thread against this end of the ribbon to lock it in place.

Trim away the excess ends of the thread. Put a dab of glue on the knots at both ends to secure them.

(continued on next page)

✿ Fluff Up a Ruff

(continued)

Place your ruff on a table. Match up two pairs of Velcro squares and attach them to the ends of your ruff.

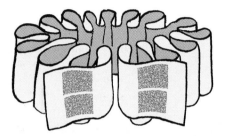

To wear your ruff, press the Velcro fasteners together. You can use your ruff as a finishing touch to lots of different costumes.

and bear empire above man." Elizabeth might be a queen, but she was a daughter of Eve as well.

Now Elizabeth faced two challenges. She had to govern England effectively, and she had to do so as a woman. Together with her lawyers, she used her wits and set about to build her case.

Yes, she was a woman like any other, Elizabeth agreed. However, God's will had led her to England's throne. By God's grace, she was queen of England, and now her woman's body was linked to a mystical "body politic," the bond between England's monarchs and the people they ruled. That mysterious link to the body politic gave her the right to rule over men.

Queen Elizabeth would rule England for more than 40 years. During her reign, Elizabeth often called herself the people's "prince." In her own eyes, Elizabeth the prince felt she must obey only one other being. That was God himself.

She might be the people's "prince," but the people of England were eager to see Elizabeth marry quickly and mother healthy sons. A palace filled with Tudor children would mean that England's people could look forward to a stable future. Without an heir to follow the queen, England could expect only trouble. Claims to the throne would rise from various Tudor relatives, and they might start a war to get their hands on England's crown.

Just days after Elizabeth's coronation, members of Parliament, England's legislative body, gathered in London. The House of Commons, the lower house, sent members to meet Elizabeth in person. Politely they asked the queen to choose a husband without delay. Elizabeth had her answer ready: She was not at all sure she would ever marry. Quite likely, she said, she would stay unmarried all her life—a Virgin Queen. An unmarried queen was a powerful symbol, somewhat like the Virgin Mary or Diana, the Greek goddess of the moon who never wed.

Elizabeth went on to wear tiny crescent moons on her gowns and in her hair. As queen she adored pearls, symbols of purity that studded her clothing, circled her neck, and dropped from her ears. She chose her gowns to enhance her image as well. They were of silk brocades or velvets so heavily embellished with embroidery in gold and silver threads and silks that they practically stood up by themselves.

Elizabeth stood ready to use her power. There was a game of diplomacy to play, and Elizabeth played it as no one else could.

To Wed No Man

ELIZABETH KNEW that she could have her pick of practically any man in Europe. If she

CAST OF CHARACTERS: *Witches and Spirits*

WHEN ELIZABETHANS thought about good and evil, they pictured God in heaven doing constant battle with his archenemy, the devil. Here on earth, the devil had his followers, witches who sold their souls in exchange for favors.

When bad things happened, it was easy to blame things on witchcraft. Milk could sour, a cow would go missing, a child got sick, or a woman might fall into a fireplace—any of these calamities could be the doings of a witch.

Elizabethans believed in a world of seen and unseen. There was so much to fear: spirits, witches, urchins, elves, fairies, satyrs, pans and fauns (half human, half goat), tritons (half human, half fish), centaurs, dwarfs, giants, imps, nymphs, changelings, bull beggers (with cow heads and bloody bones), and more. Will Shakespeare filled his plays with them, including the three witches in *Macbeth*, a play about murder. This trio stirs up a gruesome brew:

Double, double toil and trouble;
Fire burn, and cauldron bubble.
Fillet of a fenny snake,
In the cauldron boil and bake;
Eye of newt and toe of frog,
Wool of bat and tongue of dog,

Adder's fork and blind-worm's sting,
Lizard's leg and owlet's wing,
For a charm of powerful trouble,
Like a hell-broth boil and bubble.

Queen Elizabeth's people had no science to explain how the world works. Witches seemed as real as birds in the air or fish in the river. Elizabethans thought lots of animals actually *were* witches in disguise.

England's folk were a superstitious bunch as well. Spill the salt, bad luck. Spot a live snake, the same. A man gave up an errand if a rabbit crossed the road ahead—or if he tripped going out the door. Every journey had its terrors. "Some ways he will not goe" wrote a bishop, "and some he dares not; either there are bugges, or he faineth them; every lantern is a ghost, and every noise is of chaines."

In *A Christmas Carol*, the ghost of Jacob Marley wore chains as well. Did Elizabethan ghosts still walk the earth when Charles Dickens wrote his tale in 1843?

The witches in Shakespeare's play *Macbeth* **stirred up trouble and predicted doom for the title character.** Library of Congress LC-USZC4-738

✿ Carve a Turnip

MANY PEOPLE in Elizabeth's day believed that spirits of the dead walk the earth late in October. The Irish followed a Celtic (KEL-tik) tradition of carving out vegetables and lighting them with candles to honor the dead. No one is exactly sure how these traditions changed over time, but another Irish tale went something like this:

Jack was a mean, miserly man who lived a mean, miserly life. When he died, the angels at heaven's gate laughed when he tried to enter. Jack decided that a place in hell was better than no place at all. So he implored the devil to let him in.

But the devil did not want Jack, either. Jack had played tricks on the devil during his days on earth. The devil never forgot those tricks, so he kept Jack out.

However, the devil granted Jack one favor, and he threw Jack a glowing coal. "Use this to light your way as your soul roams the earth tonight," the devil cried. Jack picked up a turnip, carved a hollow in it, and popped the ember from hell in the center.

And that was the very first Jack-o-Lantern.

Grab a turnip and carve it like a pumpkin!

Adult supervision required

You'll Need

- ✿ Several turnips (the bigger, the better)
- ✿ Pencil
- ✿ Small, pointed knife with a serrated edge
- ✿ Cutting board
- ✿ Small fork
- ✿ Spoon with a point or serrated edge (spoons for cutting stems out of tomatoes work perfectly)
- ✿ Tea light candle
- ✿ Matches

When you first buy turnips, they can be hard as rocks. Let yours sit out in the open for several days until they soften a bit.

Hold the turnip root tip up. This will be your jack o' lantern's lid. Use the pencil to trace a circle around the root tip. Make the circle big enough so you can scoop out the turnip's insides. Then, *with an adult's help*, slice off the lid at the pencil line and set it aside.

Slice a thin piece off the other end of the turnip so that it will sit flat.

Scoop out the turnip's insides. Start by poking holes in it to soften it up. Then use the fork or spoon to clean it out. This can take some time. Leave enough on the "walls" so the turnip will hold while you carve it.

Hold the turnip in your hand. What kind of face should you carve? Use the pencil

to trace eyes, nose, mouth—whatever you'd like. Then pierce the turnip with your knife and gently "saw" out the features.

Place the tea light inside. Find a dark spot and light the candle. Put the lid back on and place it in a safe place.

married a foreign king or prince, his nation would become England's ally. At the time, tiny England had a small, weak army and a lackluster navy. People still talked about the time that French soldiers turned their backs on their English rivals and dropped their breeches to taunt them.

Still, England and its queen were a prize worth winning. If Elizabeth married a foreigner, then he would become England's king. She might be queen, but as a woman, Elizabeth would be expected to place herself under her husband's rule.

A string of hopeful suitors from overseas sought Elizabeth's hand in marriage. It was beneath the dignity of a prince or king to visit in person, so ambassadors from all over Europe came to court. There were any number of palaces where they could find her, from Greenwich to Richmond to Whitehall to Hampton Court to Windsor Castle. Depending on the season—and how bad the rooms smelled—Elizabeth and her entire court moved from one palace to the next, bringing along the entire household of government workers and servants—hundreds of people.

The ambassadors joined other visitors in the queen's Presence Chamber, the official meeting place for the general court, where one was admitted only after being screened by security. Like in every other Tudor room, the floor of the Presence Chamber was strewn with rushes (dried grasslike plants). Before Elizabeth arrived and stepped up to her throne, servants laid Turkish carpets on the floor in front of her and hung an ornate tapestry on the wall behind. When she appeared, everyone fell to his or her knees.

Favorite ambassadors were permitted to enter Elizabeth's Privy Chamber, where the queen, her closest advisers, and her ladies-in-waiting carried out each day's routine duties. She ate most of her meals there instead of in the large hall where the rest of the court ate dinner and supper. Of course, water was not pure, so the queen drank mostly weak ale or wine.

Each day, it was said, Elizabeth donned a brand-new gown. She was probably the cleanest person in the Privy Chamber. Bathrooms were installed in her palaces near her bedchamber. Unlike most people who surrounded her, ambassadors included, Elizabeth was fond of baths and took one at least monthly.

The ambassadors brought along portraits of princes for Elizabeth to see and letters for her to read. Ambassadors from the court of Sweden came calling with the name of Prince Eric, Sweden's future king. Charles V, head of the Holy Roman Empire, offered two of his sons, both archdukes, as possibilities.

Elizabeth already knew Emperor Charles's third son. He was King Philip of Spain, who had wed her sister Mary. Now Philip thought about wooing Elizabeth, as well. As king of Spain, Philip wanted Elizabeth—and her England—to secure his position against powerful France. Philip also planned to keep England as a Catholic country.

Elizabeth understood the games that ambassadors played on behalf of their kings. The marriage game was one of them, and Elizabeth played it with skill. Month after month, she kept this suitor or that in suspense, delaying her answer as his ambassador waited impatiently.

But it did not take long for Elizabeth to refuse Philip of Spain. Her sister Mary's marriage to Philip had caused nothing but heartbreak for England. The staunch Protestant Elizabeth would not take a Catholic husband to lord over her.

Philip gave up on his proposal and married a French princess instead. But others hung on for months hoping that Elizabeth would answer yes. Sooner or later, they thought, this young woman would do what every eligible maiden did: marry. They could never imagine that Elizabeth would stay unwed.

Playing the marriage game suited Elizabeth. She liked to play cat and mouse as 10 or more ambassadors visited her court. If she liked a man, she would remove her glove to allow him to kiss her hand. She knew she was pretty, and the attentions of so many men boosted her

Robert Dudley, Queen Elizabeth's favorite at court. In 1564, Elizabeth gave him the title that made him earl of Leicester. © iStockphoto/Hulton Archive

image. Yet Elizabeth depended on more than her looks to control the men in her life. Like a cat batting a group of hapless mice, the queen waved her slender hands and used her wits like a set of claws.

Some of Elizabeth's councillors hoped that she would keep matters simple and marry an Englishman. Several English-born men hoped to win her heart. Again, she basked in the attention they paid to her. They gave her gifts of silver and jewels. One eager suitor hosted a banquet capped by one of Elizabeth's favorite entertainments, a masque, a fancy party with scenery, costumes, and dancing. As candles burned late into the night, Elizabeth led the revels.

As the first year of Elizabeth's reign played out, the attentions of one courtier soon eclipsed the hopes of others. He was Lord Robert Dudley, the queen's master of the horse. Dudley oversaw Elizabeth's stables, which housed hundreds of horses, and he did his job well.

Quite tall at six feet, Dudley sported the dark good looks that made him a lady's dream and athletic gifts that made him the envy of gentlemen. Dudley had proved his bravery at a jousting tournament to celebrate Elizabeth's coronation. There, as she looked on, Dudley showed he could wield both lance and shield as his horse charged toward his opponent.

Dudley was a Renaissance man whose interests led him in many directions. Not only was he a handsome athlete, but Dudley had studied with the best tutors of his day. He spoke Latin, Italian, and French. He expanded his knowledge into newer fields of study—mathematics and geometry. He liked cartography and studied land maps and maps of the night sky that helped ships to navigate by the stars.

Dudley seemed to have it all, and it didn't take long for Elizabeth's lords and ladies to see that she adored him. He was smart, and their talks sparkled. Elizabeth liked to laugh, and Dudley made sure that she did. They flirted with one another, and Elizabeth did not hide her fondness for him.

However, Dudley already had a wife. True, the marriage seemed to be in name only, and the couple had no children, but for Dudley to appear to court the queen was outrageous. Yet Elizabeth and her Master of the Horse kept up

LEFT: Queen Elizabeth visited Robert Dudley, the earl of Leicester, at Kenilworth Castle. To impress her, he added a building as well as a charming garden. RIGHT: Today, most of Kenilworth Castle lies in ruins. However, archeologists restored Leicester's garden for visitors to enjoy.

their friendship, both outdoors and in. Elizabeth wanted better horses, so Dudley imported "gallopers" from Ireland. Together they rode into the woods to hunt for deer. And Dudley felt free to walk into the queen's chamber with barely a warning.

Dudley's enemies—and he had many—spread ugly talk. There were dark hints that he and Elizabeth were living as husband and wife. Matters became so bad that Kat Ashley, as close to Elizabeth as ever, risked the queen's anger and went down on her knees in front of Elizabeth.

Kat begged Elizabeth to see how foolish she looked to those around her and how dangerous her flirtation truly was. Kat's warning was clear. Elizabeth's behavior with Dudley cast the queen in a bad light. Elizabeth should marry someone else, and soon.

Elizabeth replied she was never alone. She was in public, with her councillors in her Privy Chamber, or with friends and servants in her private rooms or bedchamber. She had no privacy, not even in her bedchamber, where her ladies sometimes slept.

Then Elizabeth got cranky. She exclaimed, in a royal way, that she alone was queen and could do what she wished. The queen had made her point.

In September 1559, Robert Dudley's wife died mysteriously, found at home with a broken neck at the bottom of the stairs. Gossip swirled around Elizabeth's court and tarnished the queen's reputation even more. Had the luckless woman fallen down the steps? Had she jumped? Or was she pushed?

It took months for the furor to die down. Foreigners kept seeking Elizabeth's hand. As usual, she played her game. Robert Dudley still fascinated Elizabeth, and he held fast to his special friendship with the queen. In time, though, Elizabeth realized that she would make a grave mistake if she married him. She knew that her head must rule her heart.

Years later, Dudley married someone else.

A Virgin Queen

AS ELIZABETH'S reign moved forward, she reveled in her status as an unmarried monarch. She proudly claimed she had no need for a husband, because she was wedded to England's people. With great care, Elizabeth continued to build an image of herself as a near-goddess. The pope and his Catholic Church might have the Virgin Mary to honor, but England's Protestants could revere their very own Virgin Queen.

Yet England still had no official heir to the throne, a problem that worried William Cecil and her other councillors. The issue grew hot when Elizabeth fell ill with a fever in 1562.

✿ Grow a Knot Garden

ELIZABETHANS CHERISHED their days outdoors, when they could escape their dark, smelly homes for bright daylight and fresh air. During nice weather, wealthier families strolled in their knot gardens. Their paths wound along clipped hedges laid out in elaborate patterns that looked like knots.

It took years for these gardens to grow and mature, but you can create your own knot garden in just one season by planting flowers. In most places, marigolds work nicely.

You'll Need
✿ Paper and pencil
✿ Patch of garden soil at least 3 feet by 3 feet
✿ Yardstick
✿ Trowel for digging
✿ Watering can
✿ Fertilizer that you mix with water
✿ A variety of marigold plants (these come as
    small plants in packs of 3, 4, or 6;
    judge how many to buy after you make a plan)

Before you dig, plan your knot garden. Study the images for clues. Use the pencil and paper to plan your garden. A good start is to plant an area that measures 3 feet by 3 feet. Keep your design simple.

Marigolds come in many colors, sizes, and shapes. Some have puffy blossoms, while others have cup-shaped blooms. As you plan, remember how wide and tall your plants will grow. Think: if a plant grows

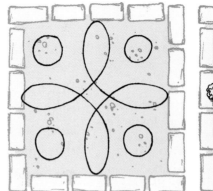

6 inches wide, how many must you plant along a 3-foot line? At least 6, maybe 7.

There's more. Do you want taller orange marigolds in the corners? Or will short plants work best? How will you vary them by height, color, and shape? (Hint: tall plants, 15 inches tall or more, will work best in a bigger space.)

Now it's time to plant your knot garden. Make sure the soil in your garden is loose and free of weeds. Ask a gardener to show you when it's a good time to plant. Using a yardstick and trowel, draw a 3-foot square in the soil. Then use the trowel to "draw" a pattern inside the square.

Following your plan, plant the inside of your knot garden first. Use the trowel to dig a roomy hole for

Herbs will fill this knot garden created by densely planted shrubs. Jeff Lewis, the Elizabethan Gardens

the plant. Carefully remove the little plants from their packs by pushing them out of each cell. Then use your fingers to loosen the soil around the roots a bit so they will expand quickly in their new home. Gently place the roots in the hole you dug and fill in with the remaining soil. Lightly tap the soil around the base of the plant.

Keep checking your plan as you plant the inside of your knot garden. Then move to the outside and keep on going. Be sure to space your marigolds carefully. Your new garden might look a bit skimpy now, but give it a few weeks for the plants to fill in.

Immediately after planting your garden, water it, but don't drown the marigolds! Early on, it's good to mix fertilizer with water in your watering can, following the directions on the container. Marigolds are "heavy feeders" and like to be fertilized regularly. Every few days, stick your fingers in the dirt to check for moisture. If the soil is getting dry, it's time to water. Early morning or later in the day works best. Can you guess why?

London grew along the banks of the Thames River, a major transportation route for the city. Queen Elizabeth knew all of London's landmarks, including the Bear Garden, Old St. Paul's Cathedral, the Globe Theatre, and the Tower of London. The map also shows the heads of traitors stuck on pikes atop London Bridge. Most of London burned to the ground in 1666.

England had been at war with France, and as soldiers returned home, they brought deadly smallpox with them. Several noble ladies died, and then came Elizabeth's turn to battle smallpox. When she didn't break out with its telltale spots right away, her doctors worried that Elizabeth would suffer a very strong case. At one point, the young queen was so sick she lost her hearing and fell unconscious. The troubled members of her Privy Council expected the worst, that the queen would die. Who would follow her?

There were a number of possible heirs to the throne. Elizabeth had two first cousins, Catherine and Mary Grey, the younger sisters of Lady Jane Grey. However, Elizabeth had no use for them and refused to name them as heirs to her throne.

The better choice seemed to be another cousin, already a queen herself. Her name was Mary Stuart, queen of Scotland. But Mary was a Catholic with ties to the royal family of France, also Catholics, and England's sworn

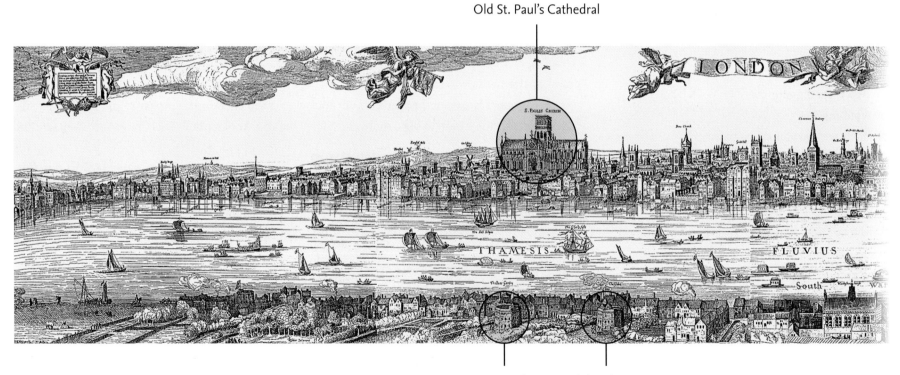

Old St. Paul's Cathedral

Bear Garden   Globe Theatre

enemies. To the strong Protestant council, Mary, Queen of Scots was a bad idea.

Although Elizabeth was nearly out of her mind with fever, the Privy Council crowded into her chamber to ask who should follow her. The sick queen mumbled that England should pass into Dudley's hands. He could serve as lord protector. Cecil and the others gasped at her words—Dudley would never do!

Smallpox did not overcome Elizabeth after all, though it left a few telltale scars on her face. She began to improve, and the Privy Council could breathe easier. Their queen was again fit to rule. For the moment, the crisis seemed to pass. But in England's north, close to Scotland, trouble was afoot. Across the border, Mary, Queen of Scots and her Catholic supporters were making mischief.

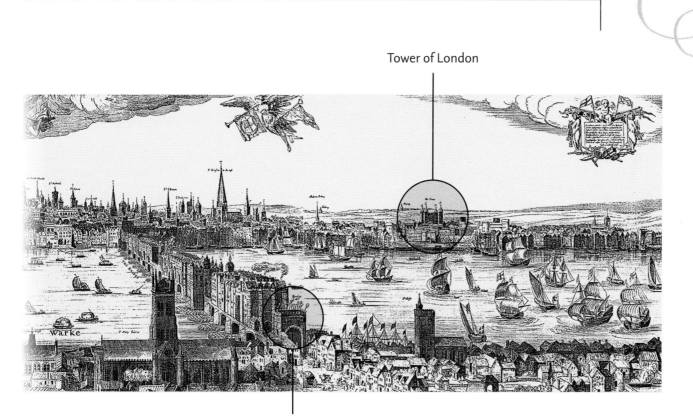

Tower of London

The "heads" on London Bridge

COUSINS, QUEENS, AND COURTLY LOVE

5

WILLIAM SHAKESPEARE wrote the line at right about King Henry IV, but he could have written it about Elizabeth's cousin Mary Stuart, known to all as Mary, Queen of Scots. In her veins ran the blood of Scotland and France, each an ancient enemy of Elizabeth's England. Yet Mary, the daughter of Elizabeth's first cousin, also had Tudor blood. Mary's grandmother, Margaret Tudor, was Henry VIII's sister. Mary believed that she had a rightful claim to England's monarchy if Elizabeth were to die. Elizabeth did not agree.

As a little girl, Mary became a playing piece in a game of nations. In the mid-1500s, Scotland and France prized their strong friendship. Both were Catholic kingdoms, and they had a common rival: England.

Catholics, Protestants, and Troubles in the North

BORN OF a Scottish father, King James V, and a French princess, Mary was only five when her parents betrothed (engaged) her to Prince Francis, the heir to France's throne. In 1548, when she was six, she was sent to France and grew up as a member of the French royal family. She went to Catholic mass, swore obedience to the pope, and spoke French as her first language.

For 13 years, Mary's mother, a Catholic named Mary of Guise, took her daughter's place ruling Scotland while Mary lived in France. During that time, the Reformation took hold in Scotland, and many Scots turned from Catholic ways to the Presbyterian Church.

These Protestants, who called themselves Lords of the Congregation, stirred up a revolt against Mary of Guise and Scotland's Catholic government. Mary of Guise called for French soldiers to help her fight the Scottish Protestants, and thousands of French troops came to Scotland.

These troubles meant headaches for England's government, because many powerful men in England were quietly Catholic. William Cecil could not be sure that these Catholics would stay loyal to his Protestant Queen Elizabeth. If Catholics again took over neighboring Scotland, England's Catholics might revolt against Elizabeth.

In 1560, Elizabeth and her Privy Council made plans to invade Scotland and drive out the French soldiers stationed there. They weighed their decision carefully, because England had no real army or navy. Their enemy, the king of France, kept a standing army ready to serve him at any moment. In England, however, Elizabeth did not have generals waiting for her orders. Instead she had to "raise" an army to fight England's wars.

The young queen did not have a warlike nature. Nor did William Cecil, her closest adviser. Elizabeth tried to keep balance between opposing sides, both in matters at home or overseas. Yet, after diplomacy failed and the time came for England to march, Elizabeth was willing to send men to war. She followed this policy throughout her reign.

With knights to arm, soldiers and horses to feed, and supplies to buy, building an army was very expensive. Elizabeth's treasury was low on cash. The queen looked to her people to provide by paying higher taxes.

In her day, Elizabeth had almost unlimited power as England's monarch. Besides, she was popular with both Parliament's members and the common people, who did not seem to mind that their monarch owned at least five palaces and had her servants rub perfume into their walls.

Mary Stuart was widely known as Mary, Queen of Scots.

✿ Build a Knight's Helmet

ENGLAND'S KNIGHTS wore armor when they fought for Elizabeth I. Often their coats of arms and family crests include helmets. Many helmets had an upper part joined with hinges to a *bevor*, which protected the knight's lower face and jaw.

You can make a modern-day version using something no Elizabethan ever dreamed of: plastic milk jugs and spray paint.

Adult supervision required

You'll Need

✿ Marker
✿ 2 gallon milk jugs, rinsed out
✿ Sturdy scissors
✿ Masking tape
✿ Partner
✿ Cutting board
✿ Large nail
✿ 2 large paper fasteners
✿ Spray paint
✿ Newspaper
✿ Feathers or plumes (found in craft stores)
✿ Sticky tape

To begin, use the marker to draw a line around the milk jug as shown in the diagram. Use scissors to cut along the line to remove the top half.

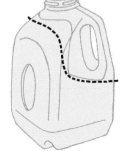

Hold the bottom half of the jug so that the long corner is facing you. This will sit over your nose to become the "nose" of your helmet. Now place the jug over your face and head.

Have your partner use the marker to draw upside-down U-shapes over your eyes, as shown.

Remove the jug and carefully cut out each eyehole. You will be left with a long piece to shield your nose. You may shape the nose piece any way you like.

Fold 2-inch strips of masking tape lengthwise along the edge of your mask, all the way around, to make them smooth.

To make the bottom part of your helmet, mark around the second jug about 1 inch from the bottom. Then cut around the line. Most jugs are made with a textured bottom; this is a good way to judge where to cut. Now cut the bottom in half as shown to make the *bevor*.

Try on your helmet. Ask your partner to line up the points on the upper and lower helmet where they will

join on each side. The points will be located above your jaws. Your partner should then mark these points with the pen.

Place both parts of the helmet against a cutting board. Use a nail to poke a hole through each upper and lower part on each side.

Take one paper fastener and run it through the *inside* of your helmet to the outside. Then run the fastener from inside the matching bottom piece to the outside. Bend each prong of the fastener to hold it. Repeat with the opposite side of your helmet.

It's time to spray paint your helmet. Follow the directions on the can, and be sure you are using a spray for plastic surfaces. Always work in a well-ventilated area covered with lots of newspaper. Let it dry well.

Attach a feather plume at the top using sticky tape. Use a marker to color the tape the same as your helmet.

Are you ready, Sir or Lady Knight? It's time to sally forth and go boldly on your mission!

But even the queen did not have the right to put a tax on her people. That power rested with the men who sat in Parliament who had to approve any tax bill before it became law.

The queen made her request, and Parliament agreed to support her call to arms. Coins collected by tax gathers began to fill Elizabeth's treasury, but as the queen grew to realize, there was never enough money. It would take years before England's army and navy could build a strong defense for the tiny nation.

One Island, Two Queens

IN 1561, Mary Stuart's husband, the king of France, died when Mary was 18. She returned to Scotland to reign as queen. Mary kept her Catholic religion but agreed to allow Presbyterians to worship unharmed. Her half brother, James Stuart, who was Protestant, helped her rule the country. However, Mary lacked the wise advisers that Elizabeth had, and she was not prepared to rule her country.

Nearly six feet tall, Mary towered over nearly everyone. Mary was Scottish and French, but her Tudor blood showed. She had the same red hair as her Uncle Henry VIII and her cousin Elizabeth. Mary shared Henry's

Queen Elizabeth and Parliament.

SETTINGS AND SCENES: *Progresses, the Queen's Road Trips*

As England's dark winters broke into longer days, it came time for Queen Elizabeth to embark on progresses. These journeys offered the queen a chance to abandon her winter home for cleaning. Rooms were aired, and fresh rushes were strewn on floors to replace old ones that were crawling with lice and fleas.

More important, progresses allowed Elizabeth to put on a glittering display of royal splendor. She accepted lavish gifts and enjoyed weeks of entertainment, often at the expense of her hosts.

Elizabeth enjoyed these revels. She visited her relatives, councillors, and bishops. She danced at weddings and feasted at banquets. More than once she journeyed to the sickbed of someone she cared for.

To Elizabeth's courtiers, progresses were both blessing and curse. A successful visit kept the queen in good spirits. However, her hosts and hostesses often panicked at the thought of how much it would cost them to put on a party for the queen.

Where Her Majesty went, her bishops, ladies-in-waiting, trumpeters, laundresses, gentleman ushers, and stable boys, to name but a few, traveled with her. These royal road trips were full of headaches for Elizabeth's hundreds of servants, who followed along to cook and clean, as well as pack up and cart food and supplies, including beds, for the entire group. In Elizabeth's day, well-off people prized giant beds with fancy

Elizabeth took most of her court when she went on progresses through England.

wood carving and bedclothes embroidered with flowers and birds.

A glitzy progress unfolded in 1585 when Elizabeth visited the earl of Leicester at Kenilworth Castle. The elegant earl planned fireworks with live dogs shot out of cannons, but that display was later called off. Another host dug a giant pond at his home and held a floating pageant with sea gods and goddesses that squirted water and extolled Elizabeth's queenly virtues.

At the slow pace of 10 miles a day, Elizabeth stopped for people to greet her as she rode on horseback or by litter. The women of Sandwich cooked her a feast, and Elizabeth honored them by sampling their dishes without asking one of her ladies to eat first to check for poison.

"God save Your Grace," the onlookers would cry.

"God save my people," came Elizabeth's reply.

Mary Stuart, known as Mary, Queen of Scots.

©GeorgiosArt iStockphoto

and Elizabeth's gifts for languages, music, and dance. However, no one gave Mary the kind of tutors who had challenged Elizabeth to expand her mind and sharpen her thinking. Mary Stuart was smart, but she did not learn to put her wits to their best use.

Though she reigned as Scotland's queen, Mary refused to give up her claim to England's throne. Mary even dared to display England's royal coat of arms together with her own. Everywhere she went, Mary made clear that she would follow Elizabeth as queen of England.

Mary's brazen acts maddened Elizabeth, and there was more to fear. Some of England's Catholics still felt that Elizabeth was a bastard and not entitled to rule as queen. Mary seemed like the perfect choice to replace their Protestant monarch, whether Elizabeth simply died . . . or was killed.

Elizabeth's network of spies kept watch on the Scottish queen and got their hands on the messages that flowed to and from Mary's court in chilly, gray Edinburgh. Elizabeth's curiosity about the Scottish queen grew. She often asked questions about her pretty cousin's looks and behavior.

For a time, it seemed that Elizabeth and Mary would meet in York during the summer of 1562. In both royal courts, the queens' householders swung into action making plans. If Elizabeth went on a "progress" (journey) to York, the entire royal court would ride with her. That meant preparations for a road trip of at least 350 people, from the grandest lords and their ladies to clerks, messengers, footmen, and laundresses. Such a huge procession over hundreds of miles would take months to arrange and days on England's unpaved roads.

As plans were set for the royal summit, Cecil hoped that Mary would sign a treaty and give up her claim to England's throne. In exchange, England would keep Scotland free of France's influence. Back and forth the diplomats traveled between London and Edinburgh. But Mary would never sign the treaty, and Elizabeth never approved of her cousin's right to follow her and rule England. Although the queenly cousins lived on the same island, they would never meet face-to-face.

New Queen, New Church

FROM THE very first day of her reign, Elizabeth knew she must secure her place as both a queen and a Protestant. Her sister Mary had broken up the Church of England and returned the country to the Catholic Church. Now Elizabeth set about to bring back the Church of England.

Elizabeth could simply give a royal decree and the Church of England would be restored.

Progress, Progress—Read All About It!

IN 1591, the earl of Hertford, who was in Queen Elizabeth's bad graces, invited her to his estate at Elvetham during one of her progresses. There he put on a party like no other and bankrupted himself in the process. Day and night, events went on for four days.

Years later, a chronicler wrote about the entertainment. Can you understand his English? (Hint: study the drawing of the event carefully for clues.)

[T]here had beene made in the bottom, by handy labour, a goodly Pond, cut to the perfect figure of a half moon. In this Pond were three notable grounds, where hence to present her Majestic with sports and pastimes.

In the said water were divers boates prepared for musicke: but especially there was a pinnace [sail-boat], ful furnisht with masts, yards, sailes, anchors, cables ... aud lastly with flagges, streamers, and pendants, to the number of twelve, all painted with divers colours, and sundry devises. . . .

Presently after dinner, the Earl of Hertford caused a large canapie of estate to bee set at the ponds head, for her Majestic to sit under, and to view some sportes prepared in the water. . . . This canapie being upheld by foure worthie Knightes ... and tapestry spread all about the pondes head, her Majestic, about foure of the clocke, came and sate under it. . . .

At the further end of the ponde, there was a bower. . . . out of which there went a pompous array of sea-persons, which waded brest-high or swam. . . . Nereus, the Prophet of the Sea ... did swimme before the rest. . . . After him came five Tritons brest-high in the water, all with grislie heades, and beardes of divers colours and fashions, and all five cheerefully sounding their trumpets. After them went two other Gods of the Sea, Neptune and Oceanus. . . .

In the pinnace were three Virgins [boys dressed as girls], which, with their cornets, played Scottish gigs. . . . There was also in the saide pinnace an other Nymph of the Sea, named Neaera. . . . [T]he rest of the traine followed brest-high in the water, all attired in ouglie marine suites, and everie one armed with a huge wooddon squirt in his hand. . . .

[Sylvanus] and his begunne a skirmish with those of the water; the one side throwing their darts, and the other using their squirtes, and the Tritons sounding a pointe of warre. At the last, Nereus parted the fray with a line or two, grounded on the excellence of her Majestyes presence, as being alwaies friend to Peace, and ennemy to Warre. Then Sylvanus, being so ugly, and running toward the bower at the end of the Pound, affrighted a number of the countrey people, that they ran from him for feare, and thereby moved great laughter.

The earl of Hertford entertained Elizabeth with a lavish water show in a hand-dug pond on his estate.

❀ Dance a Courtly Dance

QUEEN ELIZABETH loved to dance. She and her courtiers knew all the Renaissance dances arriving from Italy and France. Dancing was not just entertainment; it was a time to show one's power to visitors from other courts in Europe. Even when she was older, Elizabeth got on the dance floor and twirled about, proving to everyone that she was still physically fit—and a force to be reckoned with.

Courtly dances disappeared over the years, but researchers at the Library of Congress in Washington, DC, looked for old books of dance moves. They found the pavane (pah-VAHN) in a manual written by a French priest named Thoinot Arbeau (TWA-no ar-BO).

You can dance the pavane to the same French tune that Queen Elizabeth and Robert Dudley danced 450 years ago. It's called "Belle Qui Tiens Ma Vie" (Beauty Who Holds My Life).

You'll Need

❀ Video clips 37–40 from the Library of Congress website: http://memory.loc.gov/ammem/dihtml/divideos.html#vc029
❀ Partner
❀ Copy of "Belle Qui Tiens Ma Vie" (You can find one at www.kerrieloganhollihan.com, or do an Internet search and download a version of the song that's at least 3–4 minutes long)

❀ An assistant to play the piano or start your music player
❀ Smooth-bottomed shoes (not athletic shoes)
❀ A roomy area

To begin, go online to the Library of Congress site and watch the pavane as it was danced. There are four separate videos to help you learn the steps. The first video (clip 37) shows how the couple moves forward. The second (clip 38) shows the steps going backward.

The third video (clip 39), called the conversion, shows how the couple turns around to dance in the opposite direction. It's an interesting move: the woman moves forward, but the man moves backward. Finally, the pair puts all the steps together to dance the pavane (clip 40).

Now it's your turn. Decide who will dance the man's part and woman's part. Watch the videos to see how the dancers move, step-by-step. Then practice the forward steps and backward steps. Next, practice the conversion. You might be surprised to find that this step is harder than it looks!

You are ready to dance the entire pavane. Ask your assistant to play the music. Have fun making this dance your own.

But the new queen was crafty. She brought Parliament into the process and asked for a law to restore the Anglican Church. By gaining their support, she would expand her power.

Elizabeth was pleased when Parliament acted quickly, in spite of its large number of Catholic members. The Act of Uniformity became law in the spring of 1559. Elizabeth had been queen for only six months.

Now England had one "uniform" religion: the Anglican Church. Catholic "popery" was gone. Anglican priests dropped the Latin language of the Catholic Church. When people worshipped, they used the Book of Common Prayer. England's people listened to Bible readings in their own language and prayed in English, too.

The Catholic mass was outlawed. In its place, Anglican priests remembered Jesus's death and resurrection in a slightly different communion service. The law said that everyone must attend Anglican services every Sunday or else pay a fine.

Elizabeth's Accession Day (the anniversary of her rise to the throne) on November 17 became a national holiday. The government used this holiday to strengthen its Protestant government. Instead of ringing church bells on saints' days as Catholics did, England's church bells rang out in honor of the queen on Accession Day and on her birthday, September 7.

Parliament also approved an Act of Supremacy to name Elizabeth as leader of the Church of England. When her father, King Henry VIII, established the Anglican Church, he named himself its Supreme Head. However, Elizabeth could not hold that same title. Church bishops were happy to see the Church of England back in power, but they could not bear the idea of a woman at its head. The bishops claimed the Bible said that women must not speak in church, so when it came to religion, even Queen Elizabeth I could not do a man's job.

Artfully, they found a solution and proclaimed Elizabeth the Supreme Governor of the Anglican Church. The change did not seem to bother Elizabeth. *What's in a name?* she must have thought. Whether Supreme Head or Supreme Governor, she still stood at the top of the Church of England. The power was hers.

During these years of religious strife, another Protestant faith rose in England. This group called themselves Puritans, because they hoped to "purify" their lives as they followed God and the Bible, his holy word.

Puritans had little use for the ways Anglicans worshipped. They preferred a much simpler style of churchgoing and daily living. The Puritans claimed that the Church of England hung on to Catholic traditions, such as fancy robes for its priests and elaborate rituals during

Seventeen years after Queen Elizabeth died, English Puritans landed at Plymouth, Massachusetts. These Puritans sought religious freedom in America. Library of Congress LC-DIG-pga-02153.TIF

church. The dark robes of a Puritan minister stood in stark contrast to the white clothing, rich embroideries, and statues in Anglican churches.

Puritan ministers preached a dark message as well. The Puritans believed that people were born full of sin. Only the "elect" would earn a place in heaven, and God must choose them even before they were born. Pure living and plain clothing—that was the Puritan way. The Puritans wrinkled their noses at everything Elizabeth thought was fun—watching plays, dancing at masques, and celebrating the Twelve Days of Christmas.

Queen Elizabeth did not trust the Puritans and their sour attitudes. She preferred the ornate rituals and words of God's grace she heard in the Church of England. Moreover, John Knox, a Scottish Puritan, had criticized a woman's right to lead England. "Knox's name . . . is most odious [hated] here," Elizabeth spat. Knox's very name made her sick to her stomach.

The growing Puritan movement upset the balance among religions that Elizabeth desired. She was perfectly willing for Catholics and Puritans to believe what they wished, as long as they stayed quiet about it. If people of various faiths conformed outwardly to the Church of England, Elizabeth did not care to know what was in their hearts.

Elizabeth was no extremist. All her life, she watched as people killed each other over religious arguments. Mary Tudor's bloody reign burned in Elizabeth's memory. She had no plan to torture people for their religious beliefs—as long as they did not put her kingdom in danger.

Troubles Between Cousins

LIKE IT or not, Elizabeth knew that her fate was tied to actions of her cousin, the Scottish queen. From the time Mary Stuart sailed from France to claim her throne in Scotland, she represented the hopes and dreams of England's Catholics. They were natural allies of Mary's, because many made their homes in the north, near England's Scottish border.

In 1565, during the fourth year of her reign, Mary Stuart took a new husband named Henry Stuart, who held the title Lord Darnley. An Englishman, Darnley was also a Tudor related to both Mary and Elizabeth. As Mary's new husband, he became the king of Scots and a Catholic king as well. James Stuart and his band of Protestant supporters revolted, but Mary's troops beat them back, and Mary's half brother left Scotland in exile.

Elizabeth went wild with fury when she learned of Mary's love affair with Darnley. As England's queen, only she had the right to grant an English nobleman's request to marry. Darnley, a Tudor like her, had betrayed her.

Darnley, in turn, betrayed Mary, Queen of Scots in less than a year. Handsome though he was, Darnley was immoral and greedy for power. Within months after he became king, he made enemies among Scotland's nobles, who did not want Darnley to control their queen.

Darnley also showed a streak of insane jealousy. Queen Mary was pregnant with her first child when Darnley killed Mary's personal secretary, a charming Italian named David Rizzio, right in front of her. Whispers in Edinburgh's palace said that the queen was bearing Rizzio's child. Mary's baby was born in June 1566. Despite the rumors, the baby boy, named James, became the heir to Scotland's throne.

Elizabeth's spies sent word as the drama unfolded in Edinburgh. Scotland's nobles hated Darnley, and Mary feared for her life. Then, the following winter, Darnley was murdered. Elizabeth's spies brought the news. But who had arranged the murder, jealous nobles or Mary, Queen of Scots?

To make things worse, a sleazy noble named James Hepburn, the earl of Bothwell, kidnapped Mary and mistreated her badly. No one could understand why Mary decided to marry him.

Mary's Scottish enemies convinced Elizabeth that Mary was guilty of murdering Darnley by producing a silver casket (lidded box) of letters that Mary had written to Bothwell. The same men accused Bothwell of killing Darnley as well, and he was driven out of Scotland.

Weak from illness and without anyone to advise her, Mary lost her Scottish throne and was sent to prison. Her tiny son, just one year old, became King James VI of Scotland. The following year, Mary escaped from her jailers and fled to England. There, she wrote letters begging Elizabeth to protect her.

Mary's presence on English soil put Elizabeth's crown at risk. Together with William Cecil, Elizabeth planned a series of moves that kept her cousin a prisoner. True, Mary was never kept in a darkened dungeon, but the former queen was moved from one country home to the next, all on the orders of Queen Elizabeth. In 1568, Mary, Queen of Scots had no idea that she would live under house arrest for the next 18 years.

Sometimes Elizabeth would send promises of freedom to Mary, but often Elizabeth treated her badly. Elizabeth, who always pinched pennies any way she could, cut back on Mary's household allowance. The earl of Shrewsbury, who acted as both Mary's "host" and jailer, dug into his own purse to pay for her expenses.

As with so many others, Mary Stuart fascinated Elizabeth. Jealousy, the "green eyed monster" as Shakespeare called it, might have stirred Elizabeth as she listened to stories of Mary's sparkle and wit. Elizabeth made sure that the earl of Shrewsbury kept Mary under careful watch.

Shrewsbury had a rich, powerful wife, a strong-minded woman also named Elizabeth. They moved their household, along with Mary and her circle of attendants and servants, from

Mary, Queen of Scots's Catholic beliefs made her an enemy to Queen Elizabeth. © iStockphoto/HultonArchive

Mary, Queen of Scots designed and stitched this "Byrd of America," while imprisoned. All she knew about American birds came from books.

place to place in the heart of England. It was far too dangerous for the Catholic Mary to live anywhere near England's north.

A Rebel North and a Pope's Threat

ELIZABETH TRAVELED in southern England to meet crowds of adoring subjects. However, she never visited the people who lived in England's north, a wild and uncivilized place where the Church of England had never won people's hearts.

Trouble rumbled in the North Country. In 1569, the year after Mary Stuart fled to England, Catholic nobles in England's north revolted against Elizabeth. A pair of earls, from two of England's oldest families, planned to free Mary Stuart and make her England's queen. As they swept south, they built a ragtag army of poor men who often had no choice but to join in.

The nobles and their soldiers marched into Durham Cathedral, took axes to the communion table, and tore English Bibles into pieces. For the first time in more than 10 years, Catholic priests said mass in the church. From Durham, the rebels pushed south.

Elizabeth could not put up with disloyalty, and she sent an army northward to deal with the Rising of the North. The queen's men worked with brutal efficiency. Though some of

the rebel leaders escaped, others were caught and beheaded. Their lands and wealth became the property of the Crown—Elizabeth. The head of one noble, stuck on a spear, swayed over the castle wall at York.

Elizabeth's army built gallows and hung 500 of the ordinary rebels, the "meaner [lower-class] sort," as Elizabeth called them. Their corpses served to warn anyone else who thought to rebel against God's chosen one. No one could expect mercy for rebelling against their queen.

In 1570, Elizabeth got more news of danger. In Rome, the center of the Catholic Church, Pope Pius V had taken drastic steps against the queen and her advisers. In a document called a papal bull, the pope excommunicated Elizabeth, cutting her off from the sacraments of the Catholic Church. The pope had damned Elizabeth's soul to hell.

Of course, Elizabeth did not care that the pope had thrown her out of his church. *She* led the Church of England, which was not under the power of any pope. As head of the Anglican Church, *she* washed the feet of poor women each year on Maundy Thursday, in imitation of Jesus, who washed the feet of his apostles before the Last Supper. Whether Elizabeth knelt to pray privately in the oratory near her bedchamber or publicly on Sundays, she felt secure in her faith.

However, the papal bull held a powerful message for England's Catholics. It said that Elizabeth was "the pretended Queen of England, the servant of wickedness." In truth, the pope had invited Catholics, English or not, to commit treason and topple Elizabeth from her throne.

The pope forced England's Catholics to make a choice. True Catholics could not honor Elizabeth's leadership of the Church of England, because the pope led their church. Many had quietly kept their Catholic faith and heard mass at home, even as they pretended to follow the law and worshipped on Sundays as Anglicans. Still, the pope's decree pressured Catholics to rebel against Elizabeth.

In 1571, Parliament passed a law that brought more trouble for England's Catholics. The law spelled out that people who did not accept Elizabeth as head of the Church were traitors to the Crown of England. There was only one punishment for treason. That punishment was death.

With memories about rebels fresh in their minds, Elizabeth's councillors advised her to hunt down and arrest Catholics. Yet the queen decided to wait. She had thought about the outcome and worried that swift action might upset the balance she worked for. She did not feel ready to unleash all-out attacks on her Catholic subjects.

But a plot against Elizabeth was brewing. Her Catholic enemies had launched an elaborate scheme to put Mary Stuart on the throne. In 1571, an Italian businessman named Roberto Ridolfi carried messages from Mary and her secret ally, a highborn Englishman known only as "40," to King Philip of Spain.

King Philip believed the same as always. He still viewed Elizabeth as a Protestant and a bastard with no God-given right to be queen of England. Philip corresponded with Mary as the plot moved forward. Ridolfi, in truth a spy for the pope, acted as go-between.

Then Philip took action. His Spanish empire stretched all the way north to the Low Countries of Holland and Belgium where Protestants lived. Philip sent orders to his aide, the duke of Alva, who governed Holland for Spain. The duke's army kept Holland's Protestant citizens in line. The duke prepared his soldiers to cross the English Channel and attack England.

As plans moved forward, Elizabeth's men caught Ridolfi's messenger trying to sneak into England through the port town of Dover. William Cecil, now a noble with the title Lord Burghley, worked to uncover the nature of the messages and protect Queen Elizabeth. Torture revealed the plot, but the broken messenger did not know "40's" real name.

Then, by chance, Burghley got the information he sought. "40" was none other than Thomas Howard, England's duke of Norfolk, who dreamed of marrying Mary Stuart and

Thomas Howard, England's only duke, plotted to kill Queen Elizabeth.

putting her on England's throne. England's grandest noble was found guilty of treason. On June 6, 1652, a large crowd gathered on Tower Hill in London. Children, women, and men craned their necks to watch as the duke, dressed in fine black satin, was led out of the Tower and up the hill to the scaffold that stood above the crowd. The duke climbed the steps, said his last words, and was beheaded.

Lord Burghley and his fellow councillors hungered for Mary Stuart's execution as well. The House of Commons called Mary "a monstrous and huge dragon." How, they asked, could Queen Elizabeth stay safe from evil plots while the Queen of Scots still lived? Alive, Mary Stuart stood for all that endangered England. She had friends inside England and abroad, especially King Philip of Spain. Burghley felt that Mary Stuart should lose her head.

But Elizabeth stalled. She was willing to order the execution of the duke of Norfolk, but she felt queasy about ending Mary Stuart's life. Like Elizabeth, Mary was a queen. She could picture herself in Mary's place. Queen Elizabeth could not bring herself to kill another monarch.

She explained to Parliament, "Your judgment I condemn not, neither do I mistake your reasons, but pray you to accept my thankfulness, excuse my doubtfulness, and take in good part my answer, answerless."

Queen Elizabeth's "answerless answer" proved that she, unlike Mary Stuart, knew how to use her head. Mary continued to live under house arrest, moving from estate to estate as Elizabeth ordered.

Lord Burghley and Elizabeth feared spies in Mary's household, so they cut back her staff to 30 companions and servants. Mary complained, but this fell on deaf ears. As her life grew more and more difficult, Mary sought comfort in her Catholic faith. She also cherished her friendships with the women who attended her.

Mary also spent hours with the wife of her jailer, Elizabeth, the countess of Shrewsbury. Elizabeth Talbot, smart and ambitious, was richer than any other woman in England besides the queen. Nicknamed Bess of Hardwick, the countess made herself famous for her beautiful homes filled with rich tapestries. Bess had to pass time with Mary Stuart, so both put the hours to good use embroidering colorful tapestries with birds, flowers, and imaginary beasts.

Bloodshed Abroad and a French Flirtation

WITH MARY Stuart always in the back of her mind, Elizabeth took up other matters. By now, she was nearly 40 and had ruled England for 15 years. Her days were filled with duties, as powerful nobles and lowly people came to her Presence Chamber to plea for a favor. When she needed to meet privately, she and her advisers gathered in the Privy Chamber, where she signed documents with her expansive signature and stamped them with the massive royal seal in hot wax. Ladies and servants came and went as a boy strummed the lute for Elizabeth's enjoyment.

Elizabeth needed calming. Civil wars between Catholics and Protestants raged in France. In 1572, three of Elizabeth's closest advisers, away working in Paris, watched as Catholics slaughtered their Protestant neighbors, the Huguenots, by the thousands. The entire kingdom of France was consumed in bloodshed as neighbor fought neighbor. With so much going on inside its borders, France did not pose the same threat to England.

Queen Elizabeth and Cecil now had a bigger fear than France: the Spanish Empire. Philip was building his kingdom into the world's most fearsome power. Spain occupied the entire Iberian Peninsula, half of Italy, and the Netherlands (today's Belgium and Holland). In the 60 years since Christopher Columbus

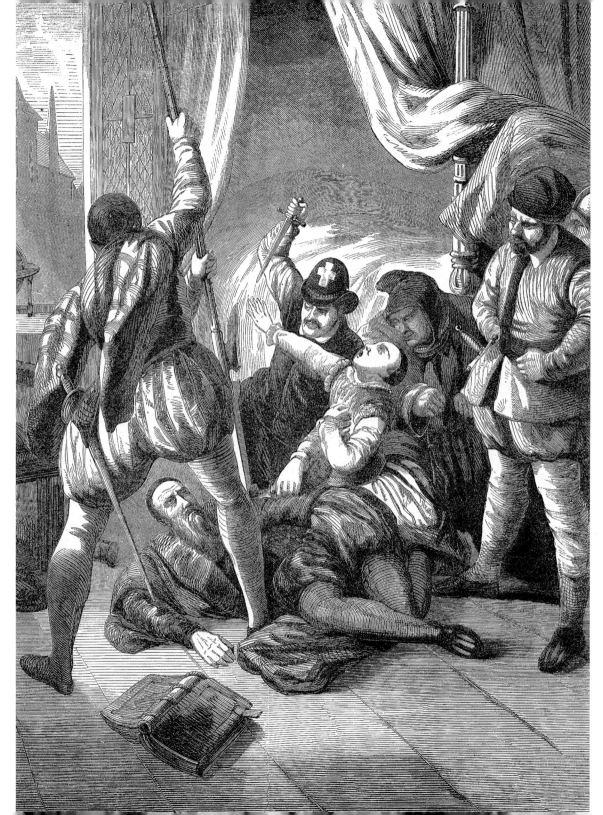

Thousands of French Protestants called Huguenots died in a massacre in 1572.

set sail for India in 1492, Spain's explorers had claimed huge territories in the Americas and the Philippine Islands. Gold, silver, spices, and silks flowed to Spain from its colonies.

King Philip was on a quest to bring glory to the Catholic Church. Like a crusader on a journey to the Holy Land, Philip cast himself as a hero. The Spanish king decided to conquer two Protestant holdouts. One was part of the Protestant Netherlands. The other was Elizabeth's England.

The Netherlands lay just 30 miles away across the English Channel from England. These "low countries," home to seaports and shipbuilders, held great promise as trading partners for England. In 1566, Philip sent a duke and his army to the Netherlands to put down its Protestants once and for all.

The duke's soldiers worked with savage thoroughness, and thousands of Dutch Protestants died by the sword. The Dutch fought back under their leader, William of Orange.

From where she sat in her tiny kingdom, Elizabeth and her councillors watched Spain's threat to overwhelm the balance of power in Europe. For the moment, France was weak. It might be time, the Privy Council thought, for England and France to become partners through a royal marriage.

Elizabeth's councillors set their sights on the duke of Anjou, younger brother of France's king. He was Catholic, but Elizabeth was willing to overlook his religion if she could bind England and France with a royal wedding.

All through the 1570s, England and France played the marriage game. Their ambassadors conducted elaborate games of courtship and diplomacy. When the duke of Anjou rejected Elizabeth because she would not allow him to attend mass in public, his younger brother stepped up as a possible candidate for Elizabeth's hand.

The new suitor was Francis, duke of Alençon. A boy of 16, Francis was more than 20 years younger than Elizabeth. He was short, pockmarked, and too young to shave. But Francis wasn't the same hard-minded Catholic his brother was. Excited to woo Elizabeth, he did something quite odd by the standards of the day. Francis sidestepped his ambassadors and, in 1579, he sailed to England to meet Elizabeth for himself.

Elizabeth seemed to enjoy Francis's attentions. She encouraged his zeal and gave Francis every sign of being in love with him. The pair spent their waking hours together. Elizabeth gave him a nickname, Frog, something she awarded to her true favorites. In turn, Francis adored Elizabeth. He wrote her love letters and made three trips in all to be by Elizabeth's side.

The match was not to be. In England, there were too many ardent Protestants who spoke out against the idea of their queen marrying a Catholic. One fearless author named John Stubbs penned a pamphlet against Elizabeth with the long title *The Discovery of a Gaping Gulf Whereunto England Is Like to Be Swallowed by Another French Marriage.*

Elizabeth could take only so much criticism. Enraged, she ordered Stubbs's right hand to be cut off. Still, she knew she could not marry her Frog. Whether she truly grieved, no one could tell. Her ladies gossiped that Her Majesty wept in her bedchamber, that this was her last chance to have a child to carry on the Tudor name. But in the end, Elizabeth sent Francis away. She would remain England's Virgin Queen for life.

Francis, duke of Alençon. © iStockphoto/HultonArchive

DANGER, DECEIT, AND DEATH

6

The King's name is a tower of strength . . .

—William Shakespeare, *Richard III*

THERE WAS no more talk of marriage for Queen Elizabeth as she entered her fifties. But her tiny kingdom moved forward. As the years wore on, Elizabeth's people came to cherish their identity as "Englishmen." (In Elizabeth's day, no one ever dreamed of the word "Englishwoman.")

Life was changing, and England's people changed as well. Grammar schools for boys popped up in villages all over the country. In towns and cities, middle-class men—and many of their wives and daughters—learned how to read.

Printers set up shop and translated foreign books into English. England's own authors churned out thousands of stories, novels, poems, and plays. More and more, Queen Elizabeth and her people could read works by English authors set in their native language. Thanks to the power of English,

Elizabeth's subjects began to think of themselves as citizens of a great nation.

Still, these were times of great brutality. For example, people enjoyed the bloody sport of bear baiting, cheering as vicious dogs attacked chained-up bears. Many villages owned a bear. Most times, the bear lived to see another day. The dogs did not.

Wars of Religion Bring Fear to England

IN THE 1500s, as the Reformation spread across northern Europe, Protestant and Catholic countries fought wars that never seemed to end. Catholics and Protestants killed each other by the millions, not just soldiers but ordinary men, women, and children.

In England, Elizabeth was a Protestant queen in a nation that included many Catholics. Elizabeth's supporters feared that Catholics would rebel against her with help from Catholic nations in Europe.

They had good reason to worry. Pope Gregory XIII, head of the Roman Catholic Church, wanted to return England to the Catholic Church. The pope and his faithful follower, King Philip of Spain, looked for ways to topple Elizabeth from her throne.

Elizabeth and her Privy Council took this threat seriously. Spain's empire and its army grew richer and more powerful year by year. Philip had every chance of getting what he wished. His Spanish army sat just across the English Channel in the Netherlands, dangerously close to London.

King Philip ruled the Netherlands, where half the people were Protestants. Philip tried to force the Catholic religion on Protestants, but in 1566, a group of Netherlanders rebelled and vandalized Catholic churches. Philip dealt with the revolt by sending the Spanish army to fight his Protestant enemies. To the Spanish soldiers, the Protestants were heretics who deserved no mercy, and the soldiers slaughtered thousands of people.

This wedding scene offers a peek into the life and times of Elizabethans.

Then Pope Gregory made a threatening move. In 1580, he sent a group of priests and monks, the Jesuits (JEZ-yoo-its), to England. As the pope's special delegates, the Jesuits said mass and cared for faithful Catholics—at great risk to their lives. Roman Catholics in England became more vocal and publicly pledged their loyalty to the pope as the head of their church. But in England, Queen Elizabeth ruled the Church. Anyone who swore loyalty to the pope automatically became a traitor to England. And there was but one punishment for treason: death.

In England's untamed north, far from London, problems of religion hung heavy. Catholic men and women, at great peril to themselves and their children, hid their Jesuit guests in secret rooms. According to the law, these families were traitors to Queen Elizabeth as well. Their punishment was the same.

Elizabeth's soldiers hunted for Catholic priests and the people who hid them. Through the 1580s, more than 60 priests were caught and executed. They suffered a traitor's death by being drawn and quartered. They were hung by the neck, then taken down and cut into pieces—quarters. Sometimes a merciful executioner made sure that a condemned man died before the second part of the sentence was carried out.

Ordinary Catholics died as well. In England's north sat the town of York, a Catho-

Bear baiting, a fight between dogs and a chained-up bear, was a brutal, popular sport among Elizabethans.

lic stronghold. The earl of Huntingdon, lord president of the Queen's Council in the North, acted on orders from London:

The earl's men, ruthless with swords and daggers, invaded homes of suspected Catholics, thrusting and porring in at every hole and crevice, breaking down walls rending down cloths, pulling up boards from the floors, and making . . . spoil of their goods.

People who refused to attend Anglican services were arrested and jailed. Over and over, the lord president's men uncovered their hiding places and executed them. People told stories of a brave little girl who lied to the soldiers in order to protect her mother who had hidden a priest.

Many Catholics died during this wave of persecution, just as when Mary Tudor burned Protestants at the stake. However, in the eyes of Elizabeth and her government, these executions were not about religion. They were about protecting England from traitors—and keeping Elizabeth safe on England's throne.

A Growing Threat

THE BAD blood between Protestants and Catholics refused to end. Elizabeth's Privy Council stirred with fears for her safety. King Philip of Spain openly declared that killing Elizabeth would offer "no harm." An assassin could strike with sword or knife. Poison could find its way into her dish. Anyone with the proper clothing could work his way into court.

Sir Francis Walsingham, Elizabeth's spymaster, posted agents all through Europe who filtered news to London. Walsingham found what he feared, as word arrived of plots to murder Elizabeth. Yet Elizabeth depended on her public outings to build her popularity among her subjects.

Elizabeth cherished her freedom to go where she wanted and do as she pleased—assassins or not. At home, she delighted in taking walks in fine weather surrounded by her flock of young maids of honor. On city streets and village roads, the queen agreed to be careful, but she refused to shut herself away from her adoring people. She continued to talk with them and accept small gifts and flowers from their hands.

CAST OF CHARACTERS: *Margaret Clitherow*

DURING THE persecution of Catholics in England, one brave woman stood as an example to the rest. She was a butcher's wife named Margaret Clitherow, who made her home in York. Born a Protestant, Clitherow converted to the Catholic religion and became a woman of strong faith.

Clitherow went to prison for months at a time when she sheltered priests in her home, where she and Catholic friends could attend the forbidden mass. Torn from her husband and children, she was brought to trial in an English court. Clitherow made an unusual choice and refused to plea either guilty or not guilty. By her silence, she protected those around her. But under England's harsh laws, her refusal automatically condemned her to a specific form of execution: a heavy door was placed on her and loaded with hundreds of pounds of stones.

Four hundred years later, the Roman Catholic Church made the courageous Margaret Clitherow one of its saints. She became one of 40 English martyrs who died during the persecution of Catholics during Queen Elizabeth's reign.

Margaret Clitherow, known as St. Margaret of York.
Cecilia Goodman CJ, St. Bede's, York

In 1584, fears multiplied when a messenger arrived with bad news from the Netherlands. King William of Orange, hero and leader to the Protestant rebels, was dead, murdered by one of his Catholic servants. Things looked bleak.

Spain had flooded the Netherlands with thousands and thousands of well-trained soldiers. Spain's killing machine threatened to overwhelm the Protestant forces. If Spain gained control of all of the Netherlands, Philip would turn his eyes on England. More than ever, England and its Protestant queen stood as a tempting target for Philip to attack.

For months, Queen Elizabeth had fought the idea of sending soldiers to fight for Dutch

Francis Walsingham ran a network of secret agents for Queen Elizabeth. © iStockphoto/duncan1890

❀ Picture Yourself as an Elizabethan

MEN AND women in Elizabeth's day wore clothes that reflected their status in society. The wealthier the wearer, the fancier—and pricier—the outfits. Rules also set which colors people could wear. Purple was reserved for the royal family, and only nobles and the very wealthy could dress in red and deep blue. It was no surprise that the lowest class of people dressed in drab shades of brown, pea green, and a pale blue made from cheap dye.

Picture yourself as an Elizabethan by costuming a figure with *your* face.

You'll Need
- ❀ Plain, heavy paper
- ❀ Marker
- ❀ Scissors
- ❀ Piece of colored paper for background
- ❀ Good-quality paper
- ❀ Rubber cement
- ❀ Tissue paper
- ❀ Pencil
- ❀ Scraps of fabric, wrapping paper, foil, and cloth
- ❀ Feathers and small beads
- ❀ Helper

To begin, trace or photocopy the body outline on the next page onto plain paper. Cut out the tracing and glue it to a colorful background.

Then, have a helper take your picture portrait-style. Print out a copy of your face and hair on good-quality paper, being sure to size your print so that your head fits on the body outline. Cut out the print and, if it's the right size, use rubber cement to glue on your face piece.

Now you are ready to dress your model. This will be done in layers. Start by making tissue paper patterns. Study the costume pieces on the next page. Cut squares of tissue paper and place over the model. Use the pencil to draft patterns that will fit. When you like a pattern, cut it out and set it aside.

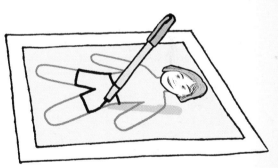

For a man's costume, start with stockings and breeches. You will first need a pair of hose that run from your waist to your knees, somewhat like cutoff tights. Pick a paper you like for hose and draw a pattern on it. Cut out and set aside. Add your shirt, breeches, and nether stockings,

(continued on next page)

✿ Picture Yourself as an Elizabethan (continued)

followed by a doublet. Then add your sleeves. Design a pair of shoes, and top things off with a hat.

For a woman's costume, start by drafting a pattern for the chemise. Continue to draft patterns for all the pieces of a lady's outfit, following the drawings on this page.

Now you are ready to dress your figure. Lightly trace your paper patterns onto the colored paper or cloth of your choice. Cut them out with scissors. Starting with the undergarments, glue them to your doll with rubber cement. (If you get excess glue on the paper, simply rub it away lightly with your finger.) Follow with the upper layers of garments, sleeves, and shoes. Add beads and feathers if you wish.

MAN'S COSTUME

Hose
Run from waist to knee

Breeches

Doublet and Sleeves

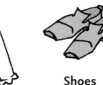

Shoes

Hat

WOMAN'S COSTUME

Chemise
(sha-MEES) *A chemise was a woman's undergarment*

Stockings
Stockings are tied at the knee with garters

Corset
A corset was stiffened with whalebone so the dress fit tightly

Farthingale
A farthingale was a petticoat stiffened with willow branches

Partlet and Ruff
A half-blouse with ruff attached

Bumroll
Elizabethans tied rolled pads around the hips to make their skirts stick out at the waist

Gown and Sleeves
The gown is laced up the front and sleeves are stuffed with shoulder rolls and tied on

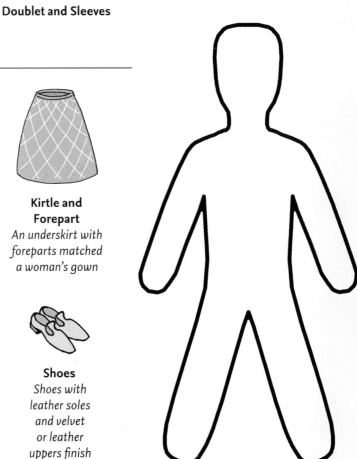

Kirtle and Forepart
An underskirt with foreparts matched a woman's gown

Shoes
Shoes with leather soles and velvet or leather uppers finish the outfit

Protestants. She didn't like her countrymen doing battle over other people's problems. Then there was the ever-present problem of cash. She would have to ask Parliament for new taxes to pay for an army.

But the Catholic menace was growing deadly. Still lukewarm to the idea, Elizabeth ordered 5,000 foot soldiers and 1,000 cavalrymen on horseback to sail to the Netherlands. Robert Dudley, earl of Leicester, ambitious as ever, asked to lead the army. Dudley held a special place in Elizabeth's heart, and she agreed.

Across the English Channel, Robert Dudley proved to be a poor choice as a commander. Without Elizabeth's approval, Dudley made all sorts of agreements to gain favor with the Dutch Protestant leaders. When the news reached London, Elizabeth was furious.

Her anger grew stronger when she learned that Leicester's new wife was moving to the Netherlands to live with him. Just who was the queen? Elizabeth asked.

An army scandal followed. In Tudor times, army officers were responsible for paying their soldiers with government coins. Many of them pocketed their underlings' pay and kept it for themselves. Angry soldiers turned up in London at Elizabeth's court to complain that they were hungry and cheated of their money. It seemed that Elizabeth could never please ordinary soldiers and sailors. For whatever rea-

sons, there were never enough silver coins to go around.

The fight against Spain went nowhere. The Spanish army still threatened to overwhelm the Protestants, as Elizabeth's venture turned more costly by the day. The queen tried to think of ways to bring her soldiers home, but there did not seem to be any way out. Like a ship blown off course, her hopes for peace had run aground. Elizabeth hated paying for an expensive war that could not be won.

This engraving shows an English lord wearing half armor, a pikeman (left), an archer with a longbow, and a musketeer. All were examples of Elizabethan soldiers.

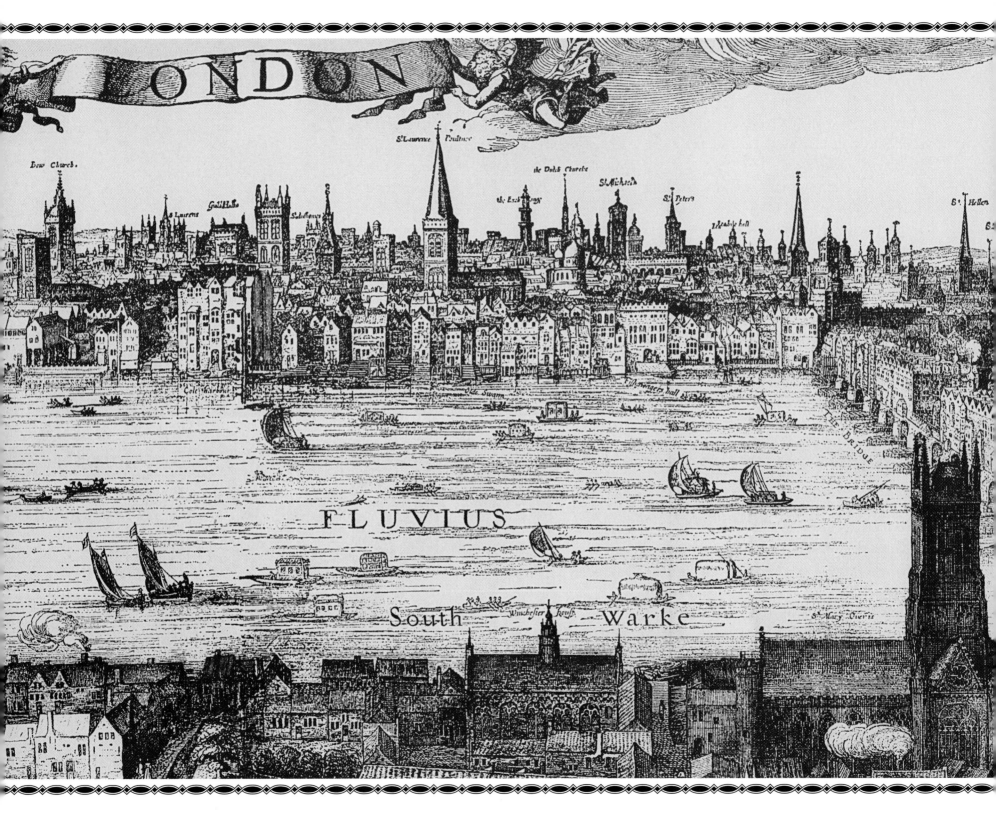

HIGH-SEAS DRAMA

7

AS LONG as anyone could remember, Elizabeth's England prized its tradition as a seafaring nation. Wave upon wave of foreigners had arrived to the tiny island in boats, and England's people kept their links to the sea.

For centuries, the English made the most of their island past, as England became home to builders of ships. Ships were key, because Englishmen needed to sail from home to trade their goods, especially wool from their sheep.

Up and down the country, from its bleak north to the south's green fields, farmers raised sheep, prized for their wool. Once sheepshearing finished each spring, inland traders delivered bags of raw wool to households all over the land. Children picked through the wool for bits of dirt and sticks and

Men at some time are masters of their fates;
The fault, dear Brutus, is not in our stars,
But in ourselves, that we are underlings.

—William Shakespeare, *Julius Caesar*

combed it with wire brushes. Mothers used spinning wheels to transform the wool into yarn, and fathers wove it into woolen cloth.

In a day when no one wore cotton, wool and linen supplied most of the fabric for Europeans to sew into clothes, hangings for their walls, sacks for their goods, and sails for their ships.

Queen Elizabeth granted royal charters to men who formed companies and ventured forth across the seas to trade. From London, Plymouth, Portsmouth, and Dover, English ships left for the far corners of the earth—as Elizabethan maps showed them. Wooden vessels, their holds filled with cloth, sailed for Muscovy (Moscow), the Levant (Middle East) and Africa. They returned loaded with exotic goods—lumber, ivory, spices, and sometimes, precious gold and jewels.

A trader to Turkey named Ralph Fitch set out toward India by land, all the way from the Middle East. When he returned in 1891 with remarkable tales of Persia, India, and

BELOW: Queen Elizabeth opened the Royal Exchange, a trading house, in 1570.
RIGHT: One of Elizabeth's ships weathers a storm.

the Malayan Peninsula, Elizabeth granted a royal charter to another group, the East India Company.

These businessmen became England's most famous overseas tradesmen. But they didn't travel by land. The East India Company took to the sea in ships, navigating past Europe down the African coast and around Cape Horn to the Indian Ocean.

The sea was a dangerous place. Storms could swamp a fleet of ships and send their sailors to watery graves. Sometimes ships would sit still for days, becalmed with no wind to fill their sails. Equally dangerous were narrow but rocky channels, where boats crashed into rocks and were smashed to bits.

Ship captains had only rough instruments to help them find their way across vast oceans. Sailors could calculate latitude by using instruments called sextants to observe the stars, but they had no way of knowing their longitude. All too often their vessels went miles off course, bringing them to tragic ends.

England's sailors sniffed the air for another kind of trouble: enemy ships. Spanish, French, and Portuguese vessels all preyed on English boats. Elizabeth's father, Henry VIII, had relied on privately owned vessels to defend England's interests against enemy fleets. He granted them permission to privateer—to work as pirates. Elizabeth followed her father's example.

✿ Sing a Song of Seafaring

THE MEN and boys who worked on Elizabethan ships were a mix of England's social classes, from well-off noblemen to street people. But England's navy built a brotherhood of sailors who prided themselves on their skills and achievements. They poked fun at landsmen who had never ventured forth to experience the dangers of seamanship for themselves. A favorite song of theirs was "You Gentlemen of England."

Check out the lyrics to this popular tune. Elizabethan sailors sang this in taverns all over England. What did Elizabeth's sailors think about their lives?

Join in with friends to sing this song of seafaring. You can find the piano music at www.kerrieloganhollihan.com.

You Gentlemen of England
You gentlemen of England,
Who live at home at ease,
How little do you think upon
The dangers of the seas:
Give ear unto the mariners,
And they will plainly show
All the cares and the fears
When the stormy winds do blow.

All you that will be seamen,
Must bear a valiant heart,
For when you come upon the seas,
You must not think to start,
Nor once to be faint-hearted
In hail, rain, blow or snow,
Nor to think for to shrink
When the stormy winds do blow.

Sometimes in Neptune's bosom
Our ship is toss'd by waves,
And every man expecting
The sea to be our graves;
Then up again she's mounted
And down again so low,
In the waves, on the seas,
When the stormy winds do blow.

But when the danger's over,
And safe we come on shore,
The horrors of the tempest,
We think of them no more;
The flowing bowl invites us,
And joyfully we go,
All the day drink away,
Tho' the stormy winds do blow.

In the early days of her reign, Elizabeth gave her royal approval to privateers who cruised in the Strait of Dover. The English vessels pounced like cats on Spanish supply ships as they sailed with goods for Spain's army in the Netherlands. The fast-moving English cruisers snagged their rich cargoes, and a good part of their plunder found its way into Elizabeth's hands.

At one point, Elizabeth took part in a plot to steal Spanish coins from ships on their way to the Netherlands. A storm forced them into English waters, and the queen's men commandeered the money and sent it to Elizabeth. When King Philip of Spain heard the news, he exploded with fury and demanded that Elizabeth return the booty.

Elizabeth ignored him, with good reason. Every time an English ship fell into Spanish hands, its sailors were made prisoners. English seamen worshipped as heretic Protestants, so the Spaniards turned them over to religious courts called the Inquisition. Spanish officials burned many of them at the stake, while others spent years holed away in dungeons.

Queen Elizabeth might be tight with her money, but she cared about the lives of England's seamen. These brave souls helped her to keep England strong and at peace. In her queenly eyes, King Philip had no right to the treasure her sailors had stolen.

The Seadogs Hawkins and Drake

IN PLYMOUTH on England's southern coast, a family named Hawkins flourished in the trading business. Their best-known son was John, a boy who grew up knowing he would go to sea. John's father William, himself a wealthy ship's captain, had sailed as a privateer for Henry VIII. As privateers holding a license from the king or queen of England, the Hawkinses had the legal right to attack enemies on land and sea.

Young John learned how to trade and to raid, the work of a privateer. A ship's captain was expected to act as both a businessman handling his cargo of woolen cloth and as a warrior bound to defend his ships as they sailed into dark waters. Enemy ships from Spain and Portugal sailed the sea, and enemy outposts along the African coast and in the Caribbean held the promise of plunder.

Hawkins traded not just in cloth but in slaves. Other Englishmen had become rich by sailing to the African coast in search of men and women to buy and sell.

The slave trade was an active business throughout Africa, where many societies enslaved outsiders to do their work. Early in the 1500s, Spain and Portugal bought people in West Africa and shipped them west, across the Atlantic Ocean, to work in their colonies.

In the early 1900s, an historian explained the beliefs of Elizabeth and her countrymen when England opened its slave trade:

[I]n 1553, John Lok was tempted to the African shores by the ivory and gold dust; and he (first of Englishmen), discovering that the negroes [Africans] "were a people of beastly living, without God, law, religion, or commonwealth..." gave some of them opportunity of a life in creation [civilization], and carried them off as slaves.

Sometimes seamen like Hawkins simply kidnapped African people as they worked on the shoreline. Sometimes he bought slaves from African dealers. Other times he attacked coastal towns and stole people who lived there. He filled his ships with human cargo and, catching the trade winds, sailed to the West Indies to sell every African who survived the brutal voyage.

When Hawkins returned to England from his first voyage to the West Indies, his ship was heavy with animal hides, ginger, sugar, and pearls. Queen Elizabeth took notice. The next time Hawkins journeyed to Africa, Elizabeth paid a good part of his expenses. Her Majesty looked forward to a sizeable profit from her investment. She sent Hawkins on his way, reminding him to "serve God daily, love one another, preserve your victuals [food], beware of fire, and keepe good companie."

Hawkins was not bothered by making slaves of other people, nor was Queen Elizabeth. In the 1500s, few people questioned the idea of slavery. The Bible talked about slaves and offered strict rules about how masters should treat them. People accepted slavery as the natural order of things, the way God had planned creation. God came first, followed by kings, bishops and nobles, gentlemen, freemen, servants, and finally, slaves. Husbands ruled everyone in their households: their wives, children, and servants. Slaves sat at the bottom of the pile.

The cagey Hawkins decided that he would make money at every stop along his journeys. He sold cloth to African dealers in exchange for slaves. Once in the Americas, Hawkins sold slaves for goods from the new raw land.

Back home in England, Hawkins sold those goods at a tidy profit. He invested his profits back into his business, and over time Hawkins became a very rich man. Queen Elizabeth awarded him with a knighthood.

The Spanish and Portuguese had never thought of a similar plan. They simply used their ships to transport priests, soldiers, and slaves to their colonies. Then Spanish ships returned with plunder to build their king's treasuries and fund the Catholic Church. But

John Hawkins. Public Library of Cincinnati and Hamilton County

the Spanish way of dealing with its settlements turned out to be shortsighted. Spain owned huge colonies, but Spain was not to become the proud trading nation that England was.

For hundreds of years, England carried on Hawkins's three-point form of commerce. Once England established its colonies in the 1600s, this Triangular Trade spread from England to Africa to the east coast of North America in colonies from Georgia to Massachusetts.

In the 1550s, a young Hawkins relative, Francis Drake, showed up in Plymouth and asked for work. Drake hailed from England's yeoman stock. His family owned land but had not moved up England's social ladder into the ranks of gentlemen. Drake learned the sailor's life working for the Hawkins family in England's port town of Plymouth. He learned his lessons well as the Hawkins family shipped cargo, privateered, and joined in the slave trade.

Drake learned everything possible about navigation and how to plot a ship's course at sea. He studied star charts and practiced with instruments of navigation. In time, Drake became one of the most skilled ship pilots anywhere.

Drake had a gift for seafaring, and he blazed his way up through a series of jobs until he earned the right to captain one of Hawkins's ships.

On Drake's second voyage with Hawkins in 1568, both nearly died at the hands of Spaniards. Drake and Hawkins each commanded a ship in a fleet of four vessels sailing in the Caribbean. One ship needed repair, so the group anchored at a Spanish colony in Mexico. At first the Spanish seemed friendly, but then they turned on the unsuspecting Englishmen and slaughtered many of them.

Drake and Hawkins barely escaped on two small ships and started home to England. Many crewmen volunteered to stay behind because the fleeing ships were so small. But these sailors were Protestants, and when the Inquisition spread across the Atlantic to Spain's colonies, many of them were executed as heretics.

To Queen Elizabeth, Hawkins and Drake were heroes. She made Hawkins treasurer of the navy in 1577, and he began the process of modernizing Elizabeth's ships. Hawkins introduced new designs. The navy's stodgy, broad vessels that sat high in the water gave way to slimmer ships that could turn quickly with the wind.

Drake Goes Global

THE QUEEN gave Francis Drake free rein to trade for England while doing as much harm

TOP: African slaves were brought to Virginia early in the 1600s. Library of Congress LC-USZ62-53345
BOTTOM: Sir Francis Drake. Royal Mail

to Spain as he could. She awarded Drake with a license to privateer, and he attacked and looted Spanish ships anytime he could.

After Drake's disaster with Spain near Mexico in 1568, he vowed to take revenge on King Philip and Spain's navy. Drake returned with his fleet to Central America in 1572. Though his major attack faltered, Drake robbed a mule train of its silver. He slashed his way through Panama's jungle and became the first Englishman to see the Pacific Ocean from America's shores.

Drake again sailed from England westward in December 1577. On Elizabeth's orders, he planned to attack the Spanish in their own waters along the Pacific coast. Captaining the lead ship, the *Golden Hind* ("hind" means "deer"), Drake started his voyage with five ships. But when he left Brazil's coast, only the *Golden Hind* remained. Storms, a mutiny, and the need for speed took the rest.

Drake sailed south and crossed to the Pacific through the Straits of Magellan in August 1578. For the first time, an English ship sailed up the west coast of South America. Clueless, the Spanish were shocked at the sight of the *Golden Hind* as it attacked and took the *Cagafuego*, Spain's prized vessel loaded with treasure.

Francis Drake presented Elizabeth with her share of treasure, and she rewarded him with a knighthood.

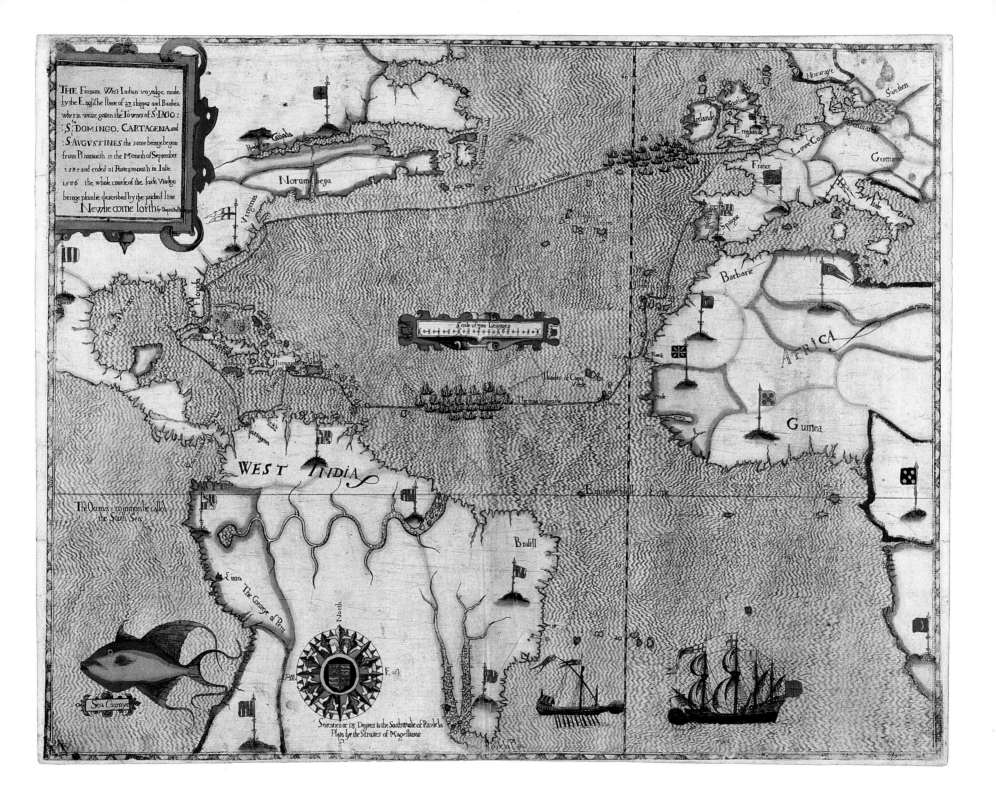

THE Famouse West Indian voyadge made
by the Englishe fleete of 23 shippes and Barkes
wher in weare gotten the Townes of S. IAGO:
S. DOMINGO, CARTAGENA and
S. AVGVSTINES the same beinge begon
from Plimmouth in the Moneth of September
1585 and ended at Portesmouth in Iulie
1586 the whole course of the saide Viadge
beinge plainlie described by the pricked lyne
Newlie come forth by Baptista Boazio

Norumbega

Virginia

Florida

S. Augustine

Bay of Mexico

Hispaniola Islande

S. Iohns Islande

WEST INDIA

The Ocean commonlie called
the South Sea

The Course of Peru

Sea Conny

Peru

North

SPIS   East

Seuentien or 18 Degrees to the Southwarde of Rio de la
Plata lye the Straites of Magellanes

Brasill

Equinoctiall Lyne

Canada

The way Homeward

The way Outward

Scale of 500 Leaumes

Ilandes of the Cores

Ilandes of Canaria

Ilandes of Cape Verde

Norwaye

Sweden

Irelande

Scotland

Englande

Lower Countrie

Denmarck

Germanie

Fraunce

Italie

Spagne

Barbarie

AFRICA

Guinea

Drake sailed north to San Francisco, where winter cold stopped him. To sail back south through Spanish waters was foolhardy. Taking his chances, he headed west across the Pacific Ocean in July 1579. It took another 14 months and more adventures, but in September 1580, Drake returned home to Plymouth. His feat was so astounding Queen Elizabeth herself traveled to meet him on the *Golden Hind*.

The Queen and Her Colonizers

As England and Spain prepared for battle in the Old World, the enemy nations also competed in the far-off New World. Spain's takeover of the Americas sparked a change in the way English explorers looked at the New World. For many years, these explorers looked for ways to somehow sail through the New World and on westward toward the riches of India. They did not think about colonizing the Americas.

One such explorer was an English sea captain named Martin Frobisher. In 1577, Frobisher sailed due west from England to Newfoundland, where he navigated icy straits looking for a northern route to India. He returned home without ever locating the elusive Northwest Passage, and the tons of glittering rocks he brought with him turned out to be fool's gold.

However, as Spanish and Portuguese ships returned from their American colonies laden with riches, more English adventurers wanted to get in on the action. They went to the queen and asked for her approval to sail to North America and establish colonies in her name. There they could harass and plunder Spanish ships from bases along the coast, as they grabbed the gold and jewels sure to be inland. Among these businessmen was one of Elizabeth's favorite courtiers, a young man named Walter Raleigh.

FACING PAGE: **An Elizabethan map shows amazing details of Francis Drake's voyage to the West Indies in 1585–86.** Library of Congress Maps Collection

LEFT: **Walter Raleigh returned to England with paintings of the Native American people who lived in Virginia.** Library of Congress LC-USZ62-540
RIGHT: **Walter Raleigh.** Library of Congress LC-USZ62-2951

✿ Make an Elizabethan Map in 3-D

SINCE PEOPLE first began to communicate, they have scrawled maps on dirt, walls, animal skins, and paper. Elizabethans favored Renaissance-style mapmaking and created maps that were works of art. Today, an authentic Elizabethan map can cost hundreds of dollars.

Sometimes Elizabethan maps appeared as tiny drawings of hills, rivers, and villages. They now serve as charming reminders of life more than 400 years ago.

You can map out your own neighborhood in the Elizabethan way—with a twist. Make your map in three dimensions!

You'll Need
- ✿ Paper and pencil
- ✿ Lid to a large cardboard box (such as a gift box)
- ✿ Paint, paintbrushes, colored markers
- ✿ Ruler
- ✿ Scissors
- ✿ Craft glue and glue dots
- ✿ Glitter
- ✿ Random materials—small boxes, paper egg cartons, bits of cloth, wrapping paper, construction paper, foil, toothpicks, chopsticks, brown lunch bags

Start by taking a walk through your neighborhood. How big an area will you map out? Just your block might work well, or you might want to include several blocks on your map. Take notes about what you see: streets, buildings, signs, hills, trees, rivers or creeks, parks, businesses, schools, and places of worship.

At home, draw out a plan for your map on paper. Use the ruler to plot out areas such as city blocks, streets, and buildings. Study your rough draft and make changes as needed. Elizabethan mapmakers often drew hills and buildings right on their maps. These weren't always drawn the right size—the point was to show they were there. You can add such details too.

Once you like your plan, transfer it to the inside of the box lid. You will need to enlarge your map to fit the lid. Use the ruler to measure the outside dimensions of your draft map. Then measure the inside of the box lid. How much larger is your final map? Think: how will you draw the bigger map?

A London map shows the Thames River, along with buildings, trees, and people.

Use the ruler to help you draw your final map—lightly in pencil—inside the box lid. Sketch out the streets, blocks, buildings, and natural features such as trees, hills, streams, and rocks.

Now it's time to think outside of the box. How will you bring your map into the third dimension? Look at your collection of papers, paper and plastic boxes, egg cartons and the like. What will work to represent buildings, streets, and sidewalks? Can you fold paper to look like a roof? Don't forget natural features. Blue ribbon or cloth can make a creek. You can twist a piece of brown paper bag and top it with green yarn to make a tree. The lid and bottom of a small gift box make a great house.

Think: Elizabethans put objects on maps because they were important to them. What's important to you?

In the 1580s, Raleigh was a rising star in Elizabeth's court. He made a name for himself by fighting in Ireland, where rebels tried to overthrow English colonies. Raleigh, clever with his pen and a gifted poet, flattered his way into Elizabeth's good graces. He proposed that England establish a colony on the shores of North America and promised to name it Virginia, in honor of England's Virgin Queen.

With dreams of gold and jewels ripe for the taking, Raleigh tried twice to establish a secure settlement in Virginia, starting in 1585. Both times, the settlements failed. The second, the famed Lost Colony of Virginia, vanished. The only sign left was the word "Crotoan," a tribe's name, carved into a tree trunk. No more English settled in North America until the Pilgrims arrived in Massachusetts in 1620.

Death Comes for a Queen

EVEN AS Walter Raleigh struggled to establish England's colony in Virginia, Elizabeth dealt with her longtime problem, Mary, Queen of Scots. The Scottish queen still lived under house arrest, watched by guards around the clock. Still, the very fact that Mary Stuart was alive meant Elizabeth's own life was in danger.

As troubles in the Netherlands plagued Elizabeth, the queen's men continued their hunt for Catholics who might form plots against her. Spymaster Francis Walsingham trailed Francis Throckmorton, the young heir of one of England's rich Catholic families, who had just returned to England from visiting Europe.

Throckmorton's travels seemed shady, and Walsingham suspected a plot. Throckmorton was tortured on the rack, and after two days he confessed to everything. Indeed, Elizabeth's life was in peril. Catholics in France, backed by the pope and King Philip of Spain, were scheming to invade England, kill Elizabeth, and replace her with Mary, Queen of Scots.

Throckmorton had even more to confess. Mary Stuart herself was tangled up in the Throckmorton plot. Mary had hoped to escape and return to Scotland to join her son. King James of Scotland, however, had no plans to share his power with his mother. Already he imagined that he—not his mother—would follow Elizabeth on England's throne. The young man steadfastly ignored Mary's pleas to rescue her from house arrest.

Abandoned by her son, Mary turned her fury on Elizabeth as a new plot evolved. Though she denied it, it seemed that Mary began to plan for Elizabeth's downfall.

ABOVE: An old German map of Virginia.

RIGHT: A statue of Queen Elizabeth stands in the Elizabethan Gardens near the site of Walter Raleigh's lost colony in Virginia.

Jeff Lewis, the Elizabethan Gardens

The sly Walsingham intercepted letters to Mary as they were smuggled into her household in barrels of beer. The letters she received and wrote clearly spelled out the most sinister plot yet on Elizabeth's life. Another young nobleman, Anthony Babington, along with six accomplices, had plans to kill Elizabeth, possibly within the walls of her court.

Walsingham now held proof of Mary's deceit in Mary's own handwriting. With Lord Burghley and Elizabeth's Privy Council leading the way, charges were drawn up, and Mary

The Lost Colony vanished, leaving just a carving on a tree.

was moved to Fotheringay Castle to stand trial.

Mary tried to defend herself but could not fight the evidence against her. Too many people had seen her letter to Babington that directly tied her to the conspiracy. At the end of October 1586, a panel of judges met in the Star Chamber (a high court of law that Queen Elizabeth used to keep order in the nation) at Westminster and found Mary guilty of plotting to kill Elizabeth.

Elizabeth's councillors and members of Parliament called for Mary's head. London's citizens lit bonfires and celebrated when a proclamation of her guilt was read aloud. But when the death warrant itself ordering Mary's execution was placed in Elizabeth's hands, she could not bring herself to sign it. To publicly execute another queen rattled Elizabeth's soul.

Frustrated and convinced that Mary should die, Lord Burghley urged her to act. Christmas came and went, and still Elizabeth refused to sign the order. But then rumors of yet another plot seemed to unnerve her. She asked for her secretary to bring her the document, and she signed the warrant. Before she had time to change her mind, Burghley and others sent it by horseman to Fotheringay Castle.

Elizabeth ordered the execution to take place inside the castle and not outdoors, so that crowds could not watch Mary die. But

Elizabeth made it clear that she preferred to see Mary assassinated in secret before any formal execution took place. She wanted Mary to meet her fate in private, quietly dispatched away from the eyes of so many. But Elizabeth's councillors would not fulfill her wish.

On February 7, 1588, Mary, Queen of Scots learned that she would lose her head the next morning at eight o'clock. She spent the night writing her will and letters of farewell. Queenly and dignified, she was escorted to the execution block set up in the great hall of Fotheringay Castle, as Elizabeth had ordered.

Mary, accompanied by her ladies, wore a black outer garment. Underneath, she wore red, the color of martyrs. Believing her sacrifice would inspire other Catholics, Mary chanted in Latin to drown out the words of a Protestant churchman who prayed by her side.

The headman did his work in two strokes of the ax and lifted the queen's head for all to see. The pitiful Mary had worn a wig, now fallen away. The dead queen's real hair was ashy gray.

Word reached London the next day that Mary was dead. Elizabeth threw herself into a tantrum. Her councillors groaned when Elizabeth placed Mary's death squarely on their shoulders. Outraged, she refused to see Lord Burghley for days. Elizabeth's secretary had worse treatment; she threw him into the Tower, where he stayed for months.

Then Elizabeth wrote to King James of Scotland. In her letter, she lied about her role in ordering Mary's execution. In the end, Elizabeth felt she had no other choice than to order Mary's execution, even if she had to lie about it later. Mary had plotted Elizabeth's own death. What else could she say? Elizabeth was a queen. A queen did not admit to killing another.

RIGHT: Queen Elizabeth signed the warrant that condemned Mary, Queen of Scots to death. BELOW: Mary Stuart's body was embalmed the day she died and put in a lead casket. A barber-surgeon probably reattached Mary's head to her body. Queen Elizabeth waited for months to give Mary a magnificent state funeral, though she did not attend.

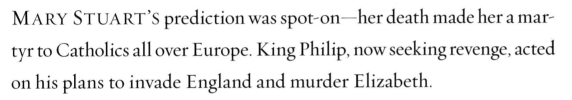

ARMOR FOR THE QUEEN

8

Then shall our names . . .
Be in their flowing cups
freshly rememb'red.

—William Shakespeare, *Henry V*

MARY STUART'S prediction was spot-on—her death made her a martyr to Catholics all over Europe. King Philip, now seeking revenge, acted on his plans to invade England and murder Elizabeth.

Just across the English Channel, Spanish soldiers waited in the Netherlands. Spain's fighting men, the best trained anywhere, were ready and armed to overrun England. They had plenty of flat-bottomed barges to ferry them across the channel and attack, but these small vessels needed protection from the guns of English ships that guarded the channel. So the Spanish army waited for its navy, the Invincible Armada, to join it.

Invincible, unbeatable—that was the reputation of the Spanish Armada. Year by year, shipyards along Spain's coast built galleons, massive wooden vessels that transported the Spanish army across the seas. Now, King Philip's fleet stood at the height of its power. The Armada set sail for England, ready to attack.

Setting Fires to Fight Spain

ALL OVER eastern and southern England, Queen Elizabeth and her people prepared to fight the Armada. "War fever" swept the country. Ships and smaller boats gathered in Plymouth. Francis Drake, back from fresh assaults on Spanish ships, served as vice admiral to Lord Charles Howard.

Other English explorers, sea captains such as Hawkins and Frobisher, commanded vessels in the fleet. As skilled sailors, they knew that much of their success depended on how the wind blew. It was good to have the wind at their backs, "windward," filling their sails and propelling them forward.

Across England, men and boys climbed hills and piled loads of wood into large piles. Then they waited. Should someone spot enemy ships off the coast, a pile of wood would be set in flames. Then, one by one, a series of signal fires would alert England's people that the invasion was at hand.

In July 1588, the Armada set sail north to the Netherlands. Its commander, Spain's duke of Medina Sidonia, planned for his fleet to pick up Spanish soldiers in the Netherlands, engage the English navy, and destroy it. With Queen Elizabeth's navy gone, Spain would be free to invade England.

Within days, lookouts stationed on the Lizard, England's southernmost piece of land, spotted the Armada offshore. Any day, the battle would begin, and the situation already looked bleak for the English navy. A strong wind blew from the south, and its ships sat stuck in the port at Plymouth. However, English sailors slid their ships at night from the harbor and sneaked past the Armada out into open water.

Now the Spanish Armada moved into its defensive pose, huddling its supply boats and

With the Spanish Armada in sight, Francis Drake and other sea captains kept at their game of bowling. A signal fire is at the back.

small ships inside a sweeping line of its giant galleons. As daylight brought both sides into view, the English could see the Invincible Armada massed in a curve that looked like a giant half-moon.

With the English navy trailing it, the Armada sailed up the Strait of Dover. For several days, small skirmishes followed. The English attacked the Spanish ships several times, but there was little damage to either side. The enemies were about equal in the number of ships, but as the English followed the Armada, their confidence began to grow. They knew that their sleek vessels would help them to outrun and outfight the bulky Spanish galleons.

The Armada reached the port of Calais in the Spanish Netherlands. (Calais now is part of France.) There they dropped anchor and waited for the Spanish army, a force of 30,000 men, to join up with them.

Then Francis Drake made a suggestion, and it changed matters fast. In the dark of night, the English stuffed eight of their poorer ships with anything that would burn and set them on fire. The wind carried them right into the midst of the Armada. When the Spanish sailors saw the flaming ships coming their way, they panicked and cut the ropes that tethered them to anchors at the bottom of the sea. Out into the channel they sailed, where Elizabeth's fleet was waiting.

CAST OF CHARACTERS: *The English Seaman*

THE SPANISH soldiers aboard Spain's galleons looked down their noses at the men who did the work of sailing them. On English ships, however, there was stronger respect for sailors who put in long, hard days at sea.

The English sailor often went to sea as a boy or young man. Sometimes he volunteered; other times he was kidnapped and forced to work aboard ship. Either way, a sailor could make himself a better life. Going to sea meant opportunities for regular work.

Still, life at sea was full of drudgery, disease, accidents, and, at times, pure terror. There was food enough—boiled, salted beef and fish, pease (dried peas and beans), and crackerlike bread called hardtack. They also drank a gallon of beer each day because stale drinking water, which sat in barrels, might make a sailor sick.

No one scolded a sailor for not eating fruits and vegetables, because there were none. The result was scurvy, caused by a lack of vitamins, which made a sailor's teeth fall out. Beatings came often, usually on Monday mornings, when men and boys who broke the rules paid for their mistakes at the hands of ships' masters.

Storms and shipwrecks also took their toll. Winds could push a ship onto rocks or sandbars. All too often, giant waves swept sailors from rolling decks and plunged them into the water.

If a sailor was lucky, he could cash in on great wealth, the prize for returning with goods from foreign lands—or the plunder he took by attacking other ships. If he proved his worth, a sailor could work his way out of his low-class status and become a wealthy gentleman, especially if he privateered. Francis Drake, who started life as a common ship's boy, provided the perfect example of a sailor who used his smarts to become a rich man of influence.

Old cigarette cards show how English sailors and officers dressed during Elizabeth's reign.

The English navy struck with their cannons, firing round after round through the sides of their ships. The Spanish, in turn, could fire back only with the weapons they carried in their hands. Their big guns sat unloaded and useless—their sailors had not practiced firing them during battle!

The English ships came at the Armada like packs of dogs chasing down elephants. Back and forth they sailed in a dance of destruction as their guns pounded holes in the Spanish fleet.

The Spanish never had a chance to use their favorite tactic: throwing grappling hooks to pull English ships toward them, so their soldiers could fight the English in hand-to-hand combat.

LEFT: The Spanish Armada formed a giant crescent.
RIGHT: Routes of the Armada.

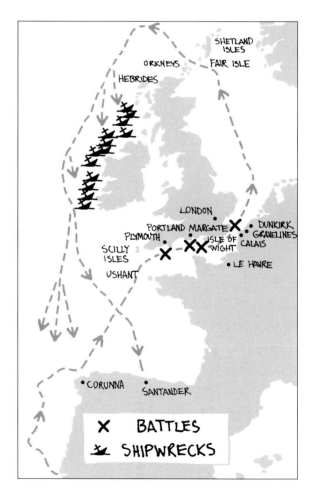

The wind made things even worse for the Armada, as it drove the fleet toward the shores of the Netherlands. It looked as though the Armada would run aground on sandbars.

But just as fast, a stroke of luck saved the Armada (for the moment) as the wind shifted to the south. The Armada managed to escape the English by sailing north. The Spanish commander planned to sail his fleet around the northern tip of Scotland, west around Ireland, and then south and east toward home.

The English navy chased the Spanish all the way to Scotland, but they couldn't finish the job of wiping out the Armada. Food and ammunition were running out, and they turned for home. The Armada sailed on, directly into a storm.

The fate of the Spanish Armada is legendary, as historian G. M. Trevelyan wrote in the mid-1900s:

The Armada . . . ran before the tempest [storm], without stores, water or repairs, round the iron-bond coasts of Scotland and Ireland. The winds, waves and rocks of the remote North-West completed many wrecks begun by the cannon in the Channel. The tall ships, in batches of two and half-a-dozen at a time, were piled up on [Ireland], where Celtic tribesmen . . . murdered and stripped by thousands the finest soldiers and proudest nobles in Europe. Out of 130 great ships scarce the half reached home.

✿ Sail Your Skateboard

WHEN ENGLAND'S ships slipped out of port past the Spanish Armada, they took a position that was windward to the Spanish fleet. The English ship captains positioned their ships so that the wind blew at their backs and filled their sails.

Discover what the sea captains knew by using a modern invention. Grab an umbrella and a skateboard to see for yourself!

You'll Need
- ✿ Elbow and knee pads
- ✿ Helmet
- ✿ Skateboard
- ✿ Large umbrella (such as a golf umbrella)
- ✿ A large area outside with a smooth surface for skating
- ✿ A windy day, but *not* with stormy or hurricane-like conditions

To get started, test the wind's direction. Turn your body until you can feel the wind blowing on your face. You are now facing the wind. Now turn around so that you are facing away from the wind.

Put on your safety gear and helmet. Grab your skateboard and umbrella. Start rolling in the same direction the wind is blowing. Slowly open the umbrella and raise it until it "catches" the wind. What happens? The wind pushes against the open umbrella and propels you windward. Are you going in a straight line?

Slowly shift the umbrella and see if you can make your skateboard go in different directions. Can you see how sailors set their sails to take advantage of the wind?

Now point your skateboard *into* the wind and repeat the process. Push yourself forward and try to catch the wind with the umbrella. What happens?

Think: how did the Armada manage to escape from the English navy? (The wind shifted from the west to the south, which blew the Armada north up the English Channel.)

Another history book published in 1895 said more. Once Queen Elizabeth's sailors came home to England, they had no pension [pay] and many went hungry.

Unlike Elizabeth, who left the gallant seamen who had saved her throne to die of want and disease in the streets of Margate [a port town], and had to be reminded that the pay of those who had been killed in her service was still due to their relations, Philip ordered clothes, food, medicine, everything that was needed to be sent down in hottest haste to [the Spanish survivors].

How did Elizabeth feel? Soldiers everywhere in Europe were regarded as servants. Sometimes they were paid on time, and sometimes not. She also could point out that, unlike King Philip with his power over everything in his government, she had to answer to Parliament. *She* was working on a budget.

A Speech for a Lifetime

EVEN AS the English navy struck at the Spanish Armada on the water, Elizabeth mustered an army to meet the invaders onshore. It would be days before anyone had an accurate idea of what was going on at sea, so the government had to raise armies at several places in England.

Though Robert Dudley had proved poor at commanding an army, Elizabeth again placed her favorite in charge of a group of soldiers posted at Tilbury, toward the mouth of the Thames River.

Gallantly, Dudley invited Elizabeth to inspect her soldiers. On August 8, 1588, just as the English navy was battling the Spanish Armada, Elizabeth boated downriver from London to Tilbury. Her advisers worried about her safety among a group of 12,500 soldiers, not all of whom might be loyal to their queen. Nonetheless, Elizabeth accepted the risk, and the next morning she mounted her horse and went out to meet her army.

With her flair for pomp and spectacle, Elizabeth played the part of a Greek goddess. She dressed in white velvet with a metal breastplate of armor strapped over her gown. Though she was considered old at age 55, she mounted her horse and reviewed her troops as they marched by. Then, still sitting on her stately steed, the queen of England made the speech of her life.

My loving people, we have been persuaded by some that we are careful of our safety, to take heed how we commit ourselves to armed multitudes for fear of treachery; but, I do assure you, I do not desire to live to distrust my faithful and loving people.

Let tyrants fear, I have always so behaved myself, that under God I have placed my chiefest strength

❀ Clues in a Painting

FRANCIS WALSINGHAM, Queen Elizabeth's spymaster, had agents posted all through Europe. You can investigate the queen yourself. This image, the cover of an atlas printed in 1579, shows Elizabeth surrounded by many symbols of her life and times. All you need are a magnifying glass and sharp eyes to look for clues. How many can you find? Many have been mentioned in this book.

Here's one: the round ball Elizabeth holds is an orb, a symbol that means she holds the earth in her hands as a sign of power.

Drum and lute show Elizabeth's love of music.
Bearded figures hold a celestial globe and a globe of earth.
An astrologer observes the stars.
A mapmaker draws with a compass.
The royal crest tops the image.
Royal lions hold the arms on her chair.
She holds a scepter to wield her power.
Elizabeth sits under a canopy of state.

Clemens et Regni moderatrix iusta Britani
Hac forma insigni conspicienda nitet.

Tristia dum gentes circum omnes bella fatigant;
Cæciq; errores toto grassantur in orbe.
Ani Dni pace beas longa, Vera et pietate Britannos: 1579
Iusticia moderans miti sapienter habenas,
Chara domi, celebrisq; foris, longævaq; regñi
Hic teneas, regno tandem fruitura perenni.

and safeguard in the loyal hearts and goodwill of my subjects; and, therefore, I am come amongst you as you see at this time, not for my recreation and disport, but being resolved, in the midst and heat of battle, to live or die amongst you all—to lay down for my God, and for my kingdoms, and for my people, my honor and my blood even in the dust.

I know I have the body of a weak, feeble woman; but I have the heart and stomach of a king—and of a king of England too, and think foul scorn that Parma [the Spanish general] or Spain, or any prince of Europe, should dare to invade the borders of my realm; to which, rather than any dishonor should grow by me, I myself will take up arms—I myself will be your general, judge, and rewarder of every one of your virtues in the field.

A witness that day reported that the soldiers "all at once a mighty shout or cry did give." Elizabeth was their hero. As things turned out, the soldiers never had to defend against an invasion. Even as Elizabeth spoke, the English navy was driving the Spanish Armada north. Once the good news arrived onshore, the soldiers at Tilbury went home.

It took two months for the news of the Armada's tragic end in Scotland and Ireland to trickle back to England. On November 24, the

On horseback, Queen Elizabeth gave the speech of her life to her army.

nation held a thanksgiving service at St. Paul's Cathedral in London, where Elizabeth again addressed her people.

The nation rejoiced at its victory over Spain, but Elizabeth gave her speech with a heavy heart. In September, Robert Dudley, sick with chills and a fever, had died. The man whom Elizabeth nicknamed My Eyes left the queen in mourning. She hid herself in her chamber, where she picked up the letter he had just written before he died. The queen took up a quill pen and scrawled a note across it: *His last letter.*

ELIZABETH, THE EARL, AND THE END

ENGLAND'S VICTORY over the ships of mighty Spain granted Queen Elizabeth a stronger position than ever before. Other European monarchs saw that tiny England was becoming a player in the game of nations. Musicians, writers, and poets created works that rejoiced in England and its queen, whom one composer nicknamed Gloriana. The poet Edmund Spenser glorified Elizabeth in his long poem *The Faerie Queene*. Many English subjects felt they were living in a gilded age with plenty to eat, fine clothes to wear, and sturdy homes with glass windows in bustling cities and towns.

However, as William Shakespeare said, "All that glitters is not gold." In the 1590s, England's economy began to slide downward. Landlords built fences around their property to raise sheep, depriving poor farmers of the

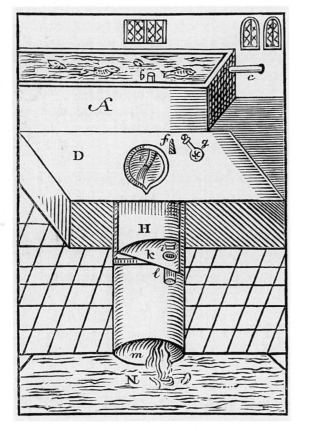

Queen Elizabeth's nephew invented a flush toilet for her to use. The idea didn't catch on in the rest of England until 300 years later. Do you see the fish swimming in the tank?

common cropland that helped support their families. People moved to towns and cities looking for work, but there were not enough jobs to go around. Growing numbers of poor people had been a problem all through Elizabeth's reign, but matters became critical when years of bad harvests forced even more farmers off the land.

There was another matter for worry. Though she might be Gloriana, the Faerie Queene, or England's Mighty Prince, Elizabeth was growing older. Quietly, her advisers began to plan for that day when she would die. Elizabeth herself seemed to deny the prospect that, one day, her life would end.

As Elizabeth aged, her vanity got the best of her. Though she wore thick white makeup, she refused to look in a mirror, and when an artist painted her portrait with wrinkles, she got mad. Like others, her teeth turned black from the sweets she ate. Still, she was fit enough to ride a horse well into her 60s. She kept her figure trim and her brain stayed sharp.

As always, Elizabeth surrounded herself with others who made her feel young. Her maids of honor, young girls from England's best families, flocked around her like adoring doves. Everywhere Elizabeth went, they followed. When the queen could no longer dance to quick tunes like the gavotte, she coached her maids of honor and pounded the floor to keep time.

But it was the attention of men that kept Elizabeth feeling most like a queen. She had lost her most adoring fan and close friend when the earl of Leicester died, but others competed for her attention. A string of men—Walter Raleigh, Christopher Hatton (Elizabeth's lord chancellor), and her godson John Harrington—amused Elizabeth and gained her royal favor.

Another young man caught the queen's fancy. Robert Devereux (DEV-er-oh) was the earl of Leicester's stepson. Devereux, known to all as the earl of Essex, shared Leicester's ego and ambition. Essex made his name as England battled Spain in the Netherlands.

Essex, more than 30 years younger than the queen, charmed her as he played to her vanity. Though he and Elizabeth disagreed more than not, he stayed in her good graces, even when he married without the queen's permission. (Walter Raleigh spent months in the Tower for doing the same.)

With her blessing, he went to war several times over the years, where he proved to be a skilled fighter but also a careless hothead. More than once, Essex ignored orders and went off on his own to fight this or that skirmish, ignoring plans that Elizabeth's advisers had set and draining the queen's treasury.

Elizabeth's wise old councillor, Lord Burghley, despised Essex, as did Burghley's son, Robert Cecil. The hunchback child to whom

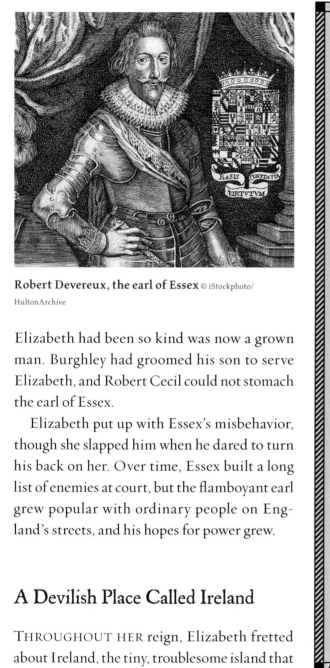

Robert Devereux, the earl of Essex © iStockphoto/HultonArchive

Elizabeth had been so kind was now a grown man. Burghley had groomed his son to serve Elizabeth, and Robert Cecil could not stomach the earl of Essex.

Elizabeth put up with Essex's misbehavior, though she slapped him when he dared to turn his back on her. Over time, Essex built a long list of enemies at court, but the flamboyant earl grew popular with ordinary people on England's streets, and his hopes for power grew.

A Devilish Place Called Ireland

THROUGHOUT HER reign, Elizabeth fretted about Ireland, the tiny, troublesome island that

CAST OF CHARACTERS:
Edmund Spenser and The Faerie Queene

EDMUND SPENSER'S childhood is a mystery, but he found his way to Cambridge University, where he earned his way as a sizar—a servant. He worked for other students and teachers serving their meals and emptying their chamber pots, which they used as toilets. Sometime at Cambridge, young Spenser discovered his gifts for writing poetry.

Spenser made his living by working as a secretary—a writer of letters and documents—for important men. All the while, he wrote poetry and attracted friends and admirers, because a good poet was a treasure in English life. Queen Elizabeth surrounded herself with men who valued learning and enjoyed the arts.

Spenser wove words into rich tapestries of language. About 1580 he began to write an epic poem, 12 chapters long, called *The Faerie Queene*. Spenser told of Elizabeth's reign by using made-up characters and events as symbols for real people and history. A strong Protestant, Spenser championed all that was good about Protestant England and its queen.

The Faerie Queene unfolds as a journey of a gallant knight, Sir Redcross, whose adventures teach him about good and evil as he seeks a perfect life. Between the lines of poetry, Spenser's readers could uncover his hidden themes—England's fear of Spain, the bloody troubles between the English and Irish, and the dangers to England posed by the Catholic Church.

Spenser lived through these events. He moved his family to Ireland to work for a Protestant English noble and lost a child when Irish rebels, Catholics, set his house on fire.

Above all, *The Faerie Queene* honored Elizabeth herself. Spenser's poem painted her as

a descendent from the great King Arthur, a leader who deserved Arthur's power and glory. Spenser's poem fit perfectly into the cult of popularity that Elizabeth built to keep her throne and her English nation secure.

The Redcross Knight battles a dragon in this old woodcut from *The Faerie Queene*.

✿ Read *The Faerie Queene*

THE OPENING lines to *The Faerie Queene* charm readers with Spenser's lovely language. Spenser laid out his epic work in 12 cantos (Italian for "chapters"). In each, he penned a series of nine-line verses. The first eight lines rhyme in a pattern that goes a-b-a-b-a-b-a-b, followed by one longer line that rhymes with lines 6 and 8.

For example, check out the first line by reading it out loud like this:

a gen | tle knight | was prick | ing on | the plaine ["Pricking" means hunting, and "plaine" is an open area.]

Spenser's words made a beat. Do you hear it?

a gen | tle knight | was prick | ing on | the plaine

Now read the last line of the first verse. It has two extra beats:

as one | for knight | ly giusts | and fierce | encount | ers fitt ["giusts" means jousts]

To modern kids, the Elizabethan English in *The Faerie Queene* looks hard to read. But look carefully. You'll see that many of these strange words look like words you use each day.

ycladd = clothed
dints = dents

bloudy = bloody
steede = steed (horse)
foming = foaming
disdayning = disdaining (scorning)
brest = breast (chest)
scor'd = scored (marked)
soveraine = sovereign (supreme)
ydrad = dreaded
bond = bound
Gloriana = Queen Elizabeth
lond = land
puissance = bravery
dragon = the devil

Now it's time to read *The Faerie Queene* out loud. Be sure to follow the beat of each line. Do you sound like an Elizabethan?

A gentle Knight was pricking on the plaine,
Ycladd in mightie armes and silver shielde,
Wherein old dints of deepe wounds did remaine,
The cruel markes of many'a bloudy fielde;
Yet armes till that time did he never wield:
His angry steede did chide his foming bitt,
As much disdayning to the curbe to yield:
Full jolly knight he seemd, and faire did sitt,
As one for knightly giusts and fierce
*   encounters fitt.*
And on his brest a bloudie Crosse he bore,

The deare remembrance of his dying Lord,
For whose sweete sake that glorious badge
*   he wore,*
And dead as living ever him ador'd:
Upon his shield the like was also scor'd,
For soveraine hope, which in his helpe he had:
Right faithfull true he was in deede and word,
But of his cheere did seeme too solemne sad;
Yet nothing did he dread, but ever was ydrad.

Upon a great adventure he was bond,
That greatest Gloriana to him gave,
That greatest Glorious Queene of Faerie lond,
To winne him worship, and her grace to have,
Which of all earthly things he most did crave;
And ever as he rode, his hart did earne
To prove his puissance in battell brave
Upon his foe, and his new force to learne;
Upon his foe, a Dragon horrible and stearne . . .

sat at England's back door. England had a small foothold there, where English settlers lived in an area around the city of Dublin called the Pale.

Beyond the Pale, the rest of Ireland was home to Ireland's native Celtic people. To the English, they were wild, uncivilized warriors—and dangerous Catholics. To the Irish, the English were devilish trespassers on their home soil. The English and the Irish battled for centuries, killing not only each other's soldiers but ordinary families in brutal massacres.

In 1595, Hugh O'Neill, the Irish earl of Tyrone, rebelled against England's army in Ireland. Essex begged Elizabeth for the chance to lead a new army against the Irish, and the queen granted her young favorite his wish.

Elizabeth and the Privy Council expected Essex to march his forces straight to the trouble spot. Instead, Essex led his troops along a crazy detour. He wasted valuable time and manpower. When Essex finally met O'Neill, the wily Irish earl talked him into making a pointless truce.

Then Essex, the commander in charge, deserted his army. With a few loyal followers tagging along, he fled home to England to

TOP: A 400-year-old engraving shows an Irish chieftain, his wife, and their household at a feast. University of Notre Dame Library BOTTOM: Blood flowed as English and Irish battled during Queen Elizabeth's reign. University of Notre Dame Library

explain his deeds to Queen Elizabeth. Without warning, he arrived early in the morning. With no regard for courtly manners, Essex boldly strode into the queen's bedchamber. Elizabeth's ladies fluttered about—there was Her Majesty, only half dressed with her gray hair showing. Elizabeth's red wig was not yet in place.

The queen always stayed on the lookout for assassins. Was Essex there to kill her? Elizabeth stayed calm. Elizabeth sent Essex away thinking that all was well, but by the end of the day Elizabeth had him locked in his room. He lost his position at court, but he did not lose his head. Instead he was put under house arrest.

Essex decided it was time for him to confront Elizabeth with an armed force. He counted on the support of the citizens of London, where he walked the streets in almost godlike fashion. He gathered his friends and supporters into a conspiracy against the queen. Early in February 1600, Essex tried to stir up a mob of Londoners to turn against Elizabeth.

Essex misread the people of London. He might have been popular, but Londoners were not about to rebel against their queen. Overpowered by Elizabeth's loyal men, Essex was captured and sent to the Tower of London. On the morning of February 25, 1601, Elizabeth's former pet courtier joined the long list of trai-

tors who mounted the block and was beheaded. Essex was the last person executed inside the Tower.

Queen Elizabeth, who must have felt like a foolish old woman, stormed with rage and grief. People whispered that the earl of Essex had broken the queen's heart.

End of an Era

ELIZABETH OFTEN said that her people preferred to worship a rising sun, not a setting sun. As the shock and shame of Essex's rebellion took its toll on the queen, the sun began to set on Elizabeth's reign.

The worrying question of who would follow Elizabeth became urgent. Robert Cecil and King James of Scotland exchanged quiet letters with plans that no one was quite willing to discuss out loud. No one would bring down Elizabeth's wrath and risk losing his position at court. Nonetheless, it was understood that James would follow Elizabeth as England's king after her death. Even Elizabeth, by her silence, seemed to agree.

Elizabeth was starting to show her age, but she seemed healthy for a woman of nearly 70. Sometimes she fell into dark moods of melancholy, but onlookers noted that she still liked to dance. The queen joined in the merriment of her lords and ladies at Richmond Castle as the Twelve Days of Christmas opened in 1602.

But early in the new year, Catherine Howard, the countess of Nottingham, fell ill and died. Catherine joined a growing list of Elizabeth's friends and courtiers who were dead. Only a few Englishmen and women could remember Elizabeth when she was young.

Elizabeth's spirit began to wither as she turned away from the outside world. She developed a fever, and no amount of urging from doctors or friends could convince her to try to get well. In a few quick weeks, Elizabeth went from a commanding presence to a sick old woman. She huddled on cushions on her chamber floor.

When Robert Cecil said the queen "must" go to bed, Elizabeth mocked his small body by calling him "little man." She was furious. How dare Cecil, though he was a friend, order the queen to do anything?

But once she took to her bed, Elizabeth knew she would never leave it. Like many people in their last days, she fretted about the state of her soul. She ordered John Whitgift, the Archbishop of Canterbury, to her bedside. The rickety old archbishop got on his knees and prayed with Elizabeth until he nearly fell over.

In late March, Elizabeth slipped into a coma and, in the middle of the night on March 24, 1603, she died. Elizabeth Tudor had ruled England for 45 years, four months, and seven days. One of her ladies opened a window and dropped a ring into the hands of a waiting messenger, the signal for him to begin the hard ride on horseback to the court of James VI of Scotland. It took the messenger two and half days to reach Scotland with the news.

On April 28, 1603, thousands of people watched as the queen's heavy lead casket, bearing a wax model of the dead Elizabeth on its top, rolled through the streets to Westminster Abbey. A bystander saw that there was "such a general sighing, groaning, and weeping as the like hath not been seen or known in the memory of man."

After the funeral, Elizabeth's casket was placed under the floor of the Lady Chapel, built by her grandfather, Henry VII, in the same vault where her grandfather's casket lay. At the end of the funeral service, Elizabeth's gentlemen broke their wooden staffs, symbols of their authority, and threw them into the vault.

The queen was dead. Long live the king! England rejoiced at the fresh start a new king promised. James VI of Scotland was crowned King James I of England on July 25, 1603, in Westminster Abbey.

The new king commanded that his mother's body be moved from its resting place in a far-off church to a new grave in the Abbey. Mary,

Nearing death, Queen Elizabeth lay on cushions and refused to go to bed, despite Robert Cecil's advice. © iStockphoto/GeorgiosArt

Queen of Scots was reburied near the south wall of the Lady Chapel. Queen Elizabeth was reburied directly opposite near the north wall. James ordered magnificent marble monuments to stand above the graves of both women. James, who had not lifted a finger to help his mother when she was alive, made sure that his mother's tomb rose a bit higher than Queen Elizabeth's.

In time, the thrill of having a new king began to wear off. As the 1600s moved on and presented their own challenges and problems, England's people looked back on Elizabeth's reign as the days of Good Queen Bess. They began to think of her reign as a golden age in England's history.

As the years unfolded, Elizabeth's name evolved into a symbol. The styles and customs of her England came to be called Elizabethan. This word first showed up in the early 1800s, 200 years after Elizabeth died.

Books, poetry, music, clothing, furniture, and buildings all bear the name of England's most powerful queen. William Shakespeare's works, as powerful to modern playgoers as they were in Elizabeth's day, still highlight Elizabeth's name today.

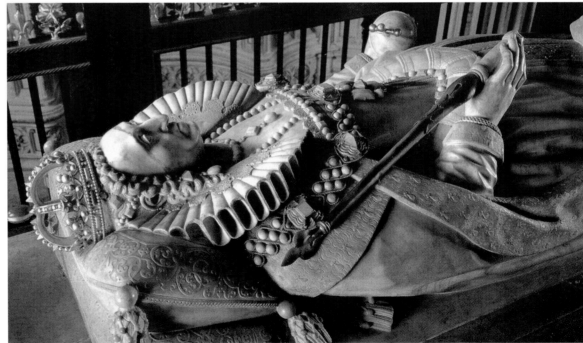

When Elizabeth Tudor was born, no one dreamt that the baby girl would grow up to rule her kingdom as well as any man—and better than most of England's kings. Queen Elizabeth I ruled with her head, but in the end, it was her heart that endeared her to her people. In her final speech to Parliament in 1601, Elizabeth seemed to predict how the future would remember her:

> [T]hough you have had, and may have, many princes more mighty and wise sitting in this seat, yet you never had nor shall have, any that will be more careful and loving.

England—and history—would never have another queen with the power and spirit of Elizabeth Tudor. William Shakespeare said as much in *Twelfth Night*. His words speak truth about Elizabeth, her people's queen:

> Be not afraid of greatness: some are born great, some achieve greatness, and some have greatness thrust upon them.

ACKNOWLEDGMENTS

MY THANKS to my editor Jerry Pohlen and the other talented people at Chicago Review Press for helping me bring Elizabeth I's complex story to young readers. I'm also grateful to my writers' group for reviewing the manuscript—Amy Hobler, Diana Jenkins, Kathy Kitts, Geri Kolesar, and Kellie Moster. Shout-outs to my son Brandon for arranging John Dowland's madrigal, art teacher Ruth Ann Siegler for her encouragement, and fellow author Brandon Marie Miller for sharing her insights about the Tudors. My special thanks to student helpers Josh Glauser and Scott Stefani for helping work out the activities.

RESOURCES

EXPLORE THE life and times of Queen Elizabeth I through books, music, historic sites, and websites.

Books and Audio

Aagesen, Colleen and Margie Blumberg. *Shakespeare for Kids: His Life and Times with 21 Activities*. Chicago Review Press: 1999.

Carley, Isabel McNeill. *Renaissance Dances: For Dancers Young and Old: With Accompaniment for Piano, Recorder and Percussion*. Warner Bros: 2000. (Includes a CD, music scores, and dance instructions)

Chrisp, Peter. *Shakespeare*. DK Publishing: 2002.

Dubosarsky, Ursula. *The Word Snoop: A Wild and Witty Tour of the English Language*. Dial Books: 2009.

Green, Robert. *Queen Elizabeth I*. Franklin Watts: 1997.

Hinds, Kathryn. *Elizabeth and Her Court*. Benchmark Books: 2007.

Hinds, Kathryn. *The City*. Benchmark Books: 2007.

Klausner, Janet. *Talk About English: How Words Travel and Change.* Thomas Y. Crowell: 1990.

Lace, William W. *Elizabeth I and Her Court.* Lucent Books: 2003.

Macdonald, Fiona. *The Reformation: Events and Outcomes.* Raintree Steck-Vaughn: 2003.

Morley, Jacqueline. A *Shakespearean Theater.* Peter Bedrick Books: 2003.

Prum, Deborah Mazzotta. *Rats, Bulls, and Flying Machines: A History of the Renaissance and Reformation.* Core Knowledge Foundation: 1999.

Shakespeare for Children (*A Midsummer Night's Dream* and *Taming of the Shrew*) as told by Jim Weiss. Greathall Productions: 1995. (CD)

Thomas, Jane Resh. *Behind the Mask: The Life of Queen Elizabeth I.* Clarion Books: 1998.

Places to Visit, in Person or Online

In the United States and Canada

Bard on the Beach Shakespeare Festival (www .bardonthebeach.org) in Vancouver, British Columbia, provides opportunities for students, teachers, and lifelong learners to enhance their experience of Shakespeare's plays through performances, workshops, downloadable resources, and special events, including a summer workshop for kids eight and up.

The Elizabethan Gardens (www.elizabethan gardens.org) on North Carolina's Outer Banks offers year-round family events with an Elizabethan flavor. Highlights include:

A thatched-roof, 16th-century-style gazebo that overlooks Roanoke Sound
A marble statue of Virginia Dare, the first European child born in Virginia
An ancient live oak thought to be more than 400 years old
The Shakespearean Herb Garden
The Queen's Rose Garden
The world's largest bronze statue of Queen Elizabeth I

The Folger Shakespeare Library (www.folger .edu) in Washington, DC, houses the world's largest and finest collection of Shakespeare materials and major collections of other Renaissance works. The Folger serves families with plays and other activities for young people and their teachers.

Fort Raleigh National Historic Site (www.nps .gov/fora) in Manteo, North Carolina, is home to the Lost Colony of Virginia. This small wooded property also served as a haven for runaway slaves during the Civil War.

The Stratford Shakespeare Festival (www.stratfordfestival.ca) in Stratford, Ontario, aims to set the standard for classical theater in North America by performing thought-provoking productions of Shakespeare's plays and other classics.

In the United Kingdom

The following places associated with Queen Elizabeth I's life and times are all open to the public. Their websites offer histories, research tools, photos, and details to plan a visit.

Hardwick Hall (www.nationaltrust.org.uk /main/w-hardwickhall)

Kenilworth Castle (www.english-heritage.org .uk/daysout/properties/kenilworth-castle)

National Portrait Gallery (www.npg.org.uk)

Tower of London (www.hrp.org.uk/towerof london)

Westminster Abbey (www.westminster-abbey .org)

Windsor Castle (www.royal.gov.uk/TheRoyal Residences/WindsorCastle/WindsorCastle .aspx)

On the Web

The British Broadcasting Corporation (BBC)
www.bbc.co.uk
The British Broadcasting Corporation, run by the British government, has an excellent website about British history and offers many interactive web features.

Work with the British History Timeline at www.bbc.co.uk/history/british /launch_tl_british.shtml.

The BBC also offers audio clips for younger kids to listen in on Tudor history at www.bbc .co.uk/schoolradio/subjects/history/tudors /sketches_clips/elizabeth_I.

Take a deep dive into Tudor history at www .bbc.co.uk/history/british/tudors (for older readers).

Elizabethan Costume Page
www.elizabethancostume.net
This delightful website offers scores of tips and links on how to dress like an Elizabethan.

Folger Shakespeare Library— Shakespeare for Kids
www.folger.edu/Content/Teach-and-Learn /Shakespeare-for-Kids
Located in Washington, DC, the library houses the world's largest collection of William Shakespeare's materials and other rare

books from the Renaissance. The kids' section of their website offers access to this collection, as well as Shakespeare-related games, puzzles, quizzes, art, and more.

Royal Paper Dolls

www.royalpaperdolls.com
Royal paper dolls are free for download on this website, which presents King Henry VIII and each of his six wives.

Tudor Britain

www.tudorbritain.org
The Victoria & Albert Museum in London has a fun, interactive website about life under the Tudors.

The Tudors

www.royal.gov.uk/HistoryoftheMonarchy/Kings andQueensofEngland/TheTudors/TheTudors.aspx
The British Monarchy tells its story on its own website about the monarchs of England, Scotland, and the United Kingdom. The story begins in 400 AD and extends to the present day.

**Time Team America—
Fort Raleigh, North Carolina**

www.pbs.org/opb/timeteam/sites/ft_raleigh
From PBS, this website includes an online video about Walter Raleigh's doomed colony in Virginia.

INDEX

Page numbers in *italics* indicate pictures. Queen Elizabeth I is abbreviated as QE.

herb gardens, 55

Hertford, earl of, 65

House of Commons, 48

Howard, Catherine, 7, 115

Howard, Charles, 100

Howard, Thomas (duke of Norfolk),
　71–72

Huguenots, 73

Huntingdon, earl of, 79

I

Imperial Crown, 45

indulgences, 10

Inquisition, 88, 90

Ireland
　map, 16
　war with England, 111, 113

J

Jack-o-Lanterns (activity), 50

James I, King (England), 115–16, 117

James V, King (Scotland), 60

James VI, King (Scotland), 69, 114,
　115–16

Jesuits, 79

K

Kenilworth Castle, 53, 63

knight's helmet (activity), 61

knot gardens (activity), 55

Knox, John, 68

L

Leicester, earl of. See Dudley, Robert

literacy, 18, 77–78

London, England, map, 56–57, 84, 94

London Bridge, 56–57

Lost Colony of Virginia, 95, 96

lutes, 19

Luther, Martin, 10–11

Lutheranism, 10–11

M

Macbeth (Shakespeare), 49

madrigals (activity), 19

mapmaking (activity), 94

marchpane (activity), 24

marriage, politics and, 48, 51–52, 54,
　56, 74

martyrs, 80, 99

Mary, Queen of Scots (Mary Stuart)
　execution, 97
　family, 59–60, 62, 68–69
　as heir to throne, 56–57
　murder plot, 95
　QE and, 64, 68–70, 72, 95–97
　tomb of, 115–16

Mary I, Queen. See Tudor, Mary

Mary of Guise, 60

marzipan (activity), 24

Maundy Thursday, 70

Medina Sidonia, duke of, 100

music, 19

N

names and titles, 36

Native Americans, 93

navy of England, 90, 100–103, 104,
　106

Netherlands
　Spain and, 73–74, 78, 81, 83
　trading potential, 74

New World, 93

Nine Men's Morris (activity), 35

Norfolk, duke of (Thomas Howard),
　71–72

North Country, of England, 70

O

O'Neill, Hugh (earl of Tyrone), 113

P

pageants, 43

Pale, the (Ireland), 113

Parliament, 62

Parr, Katherine
　Henry VIII and, 7
　pictured, 4, 21
　Seymour and, 21, 23

pastimes, 19

pavane, 66

peers, 36

Philip I, King, 34

Philip II, King
　expansion of Spain, 73–74, 78, 81

Also Available from Chicago Review Press

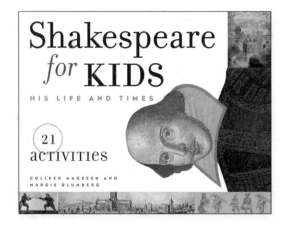

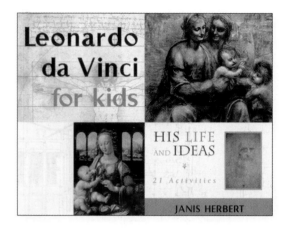

Shakespeare for Kids
His Life and Times, 21 Activities
By Colleen Aagesen and Margie Blumberg

ages 9 & up

A Stage and Screen Book Club selection

"Attention, teachers: Here is a refreshing resource to help you introduce your students to Shakespeare."

—KLIATT

"Even young children can capture an interest in Shakespeare."

—Favorite Resources for Catholic Homeschoolers

"A delightful mixture of biography, history, culture, and creativity . . . cleverly structured."

—Duke Gifted Letter

ISBN 9781556523472

$16.95 (CAN $25.95)

Available at your favorite bookstore,
(800) 888-4741,
or www.chicagoreviewpress.com

Isaac Newton and Physics for Kids
His Life and Ideas with 21 Activities
By Kerrie Logan Hollihan

ages 9 & up

"Hollihan introduces readers to the scientific brilliance, as well as the social isolation, of this giant figure, blending a readable narrative with an attractive format that incorporates maps, diagrams, historical photographs, and physics activities."

—Booklist

"Written for children, this book is also a great resource for teachers and parents."

—Connect

"Sanitized, sculpted, and politically correct stories of human luminaries are typically fed to schoolchildren. Author Kerrie Logan Hollihan, however, offers middle-grade readers a refreshing and comprehensive look at the man touted as the greatest scientist who ever lived."

—BookLoons

ISBN 9781556527784

$16.95 (CAN $18.95)

Leonardo da Vinci for Kids
His Life and Ideas, 21 Activities
By Janis Herbert

ages 9 & up

"Enthusiastically recommended."

—Favorite Resources for Catholic Homeschoolers

"One of a series of terrific history-based activity books."

—Home Education Magazine

"Beautifully illustrated. . . . Can stimulate lesson plans and thematic units to engage and stimulate children throughout a long, hot summer."

—Texas Child Care

ISBN 9781556522987

$17.95 (CAN $19.95)

CHICAGO REVIEW PRESS

Distributed by IPG
www.ipgbook.com

www.chicagoreviewpress.com